INSIDE
YOUR RIDE

Mental Skills for Being Happy
and Successful with Your Horse

TONYA JOHNSTON, MA

EQUINE
NETWORK
Boulder, CO

Active Interest Media
DBA Equine Network
2520 55th Street, Suite 210
Boulder, CO 80301
303-625-1600
www.equisearch.com

VP, Group Publishing Director: Tom Winsor
Editorial Director: Cathy Laws
Managing Editor: Amy Herdy

Cover Design: Abby McDougall
Book Design: Sandra Jonas

Order by calling 800-952-5813 or online at www.HorseBooksEtc.com.

Printed in the United States of America
17 16 15 14 13 12   2 3 4 5 6

Publisher's Cataloging-in-Publication Data
Johnston, Tonya.
   Inside your ride : mental skills for being happy and successful with your horse / Tonya Johnston — Boulder, CO : Equine Network, 2012.
   p. : ill. ; cm.
   ISBN: 9781929164615
1. Horsemanship.
SF309 .J6395   2012 798.24 — dc23
2012935483

To my daughter,
Sophia Rose

And to my mom and dad
for all their love and support

Contents

Foreword

As a rider, I have reached the top in all three Olympic equestrian disciplines: show jumping, dressage, and eventing. I only wish that in my youth, there had been a book like *Inside Your Ride* by mental skills coach Tonya Johnston. I taught myself about mental preparation through trial and error, a process that could have been streamlined with Tonya's help. Her extensive education, knowledge of equestrian sport as a rider and competitor, experience with equestrian athletes as well as athletes from a wide range of sports, and her passion for her work all combine to offer a unique set of skills rarely equaled today. Tonya is able to tailor mental skills and preparation routines for riders so they can maximize their physical talents, accomplish their goals, and better handle the challenges of equestrian sport.

I wholeheartedly believe in the importance of sport psychology for athletes of all ages and levels. Visualization, for example, is such an amazing tool to use prior to any competition. I remember watching the 1984 Winter Olympics during slalom skiing, and the two Mahre brothers, Phil and Steve, were caught on camera as they prepared for their runs. Both were sitting on the hill together with their eyes shut, gesturing back and forth with their hands as they imagined themselves actually skiing the gates. It looked pretty odd if you didn't know what they were doing, but it was apparent to me that they were visualizing their runs. Almost as a testament to the value of their mental practice, they went right out and got it done— Phil won the gold medal, and Steve, the silver!

My belief in the importance of mental preparation also motivated me to use mental skills in my own riding and competing. A good example involves the American Jumping Derby, which we used to have in Newport, Rhode Island. There were about twenty-three efforts in that derby—it was something. I had a lot of success there, and in fact, I won it three times on three different horses. I distinctly remember that my mental practice had a lot to do with it.

I had the course diagram ahead of time because it was always the same, so I started studying it a few days prior to the class. I can remember my specific preparation the night before, especially the imagery. It was a long course—about a three-minute time allowed— so many decisions had to be made, and it was important to really know your plan. My visualization would continue right up to the class, until I almost felt like I owned that place. It was so useful for me as a rider and competitor, and a terrific example of visualization working at its finest.

If you're interested in developing your own mental skills, you have found the right book—and the right person. I have seen Tonya's work firsthand, and I know that she can help you be more successful. I'm sure that this book will give you many insights, ideas, and skills to use right away in your own riding. Good luck!

—Bernie Traurig, rider, clinician, and Founder/President, Equestriancoach.com

Acknowledgments

My deepest appreciation to the clients I have both worked with and learned from over the years, and to all the horses that have given wings to my dreams.

A special thank-you to the riders, trainers, and clinicians who took the time to be part of the book. Their mental strengths and insights are truly inspiring, and their willingness to share them is a testament to their passion for equestrian sport. My thanks to Missy Clark, Andre Dignelli, Margie Engle, John French, Leslie Howard, Susan Hutchison, Courtney King-Dye, Laura Kraut, Anne Kursinski, Stacia Madden, Debbie McDonald, Gina Miles, Michael Page, Guenter Seidel, Melanie Smith Taylor, Bernie Traurig, and McLain Ward.

With gratitude to Mrs. Johnston, my first riding instructor when I was five years old, and Mrs. Wilson, my high school psychology teacher, for instilling the belief in me that true confidence is an inside job.

Thank you to the many people who contributed their beautiful photography to the book or modeled for it: Tarni Bell, Hannah Biggs, Julie Blaney, Robyn McAndrews Burton, Deb Dawson, Nancy Dias, Sarah Draxton, Kindra Ericksen, Carol Farrow, Erin Gilmore, Hope Glynn, Jill Humphrey, Nancy Jaffer, Amber Levine, Helen

McEvoy, Jordan McNabb, Gail Morey, Kaitlin Perry, Ryan Anne Polli, Michelle Spadone, Michelle Tobin, Madeleine Todd, Emma Townsend, Genay Vaughn, Michele Vaughn, and Nicole Young. Additional thanks to Sonoma Valley Stables, Leone Equestrians, and Starr Vaughn Equestrian Inc.

Thank you to my publisher, Active Interest Media, for giving a first-time author a leg up, and most of all to my editor, Amy Herdy, for her fantastic work, guidance, and encouragement. My thanks to Sandra Jonas for her amazing design skills, as well as Abby Mc-Dougall for creating the perfect cover.

Finally, my deepest appreciation to my friends and family for their optimism and unwavering belief in me, especially to those who took the time to read and comment on early drafts. I had a lot of fun writing this book, and it was wonderful to share the process with them. With special thanks to Mike McLaughlin, Becca Prager, Erin Gilmore, and Alison Rhodius.

Introduction

When I was in the first grade, I lived for Friday afternoons. I would sit in my classroom watching the clock creep slowly to 3 p.m., barely able to focus on anything else. When the bell rang, I would bolt out of school to my mom's waiting car and off we would go to heaven on earth: the barn.

Nothing else even came close to the joy my riding lesson promised week in and week out. Sitting in the backseat, I would daydream the miles away, imagining jumping the fences and stone walls we drove by. I didn't know which pony I would ride, or what would happen that day, but I was always 100 percent confident that it would be the best sixty minutes of my week. Even now, recalling the excitement I felt as I rushed into the barn brings a smile to my face.

Chances are you remember the time in your life when you first longed to ride a horse. At that moment, when you realized you wanted to know how to become a true partner with an animal so much larger and more powerful than you, a special transformation occurred: You became a "horse person."

Many theories expound on the magic of riding a horse, but luckily, we don't need to understand it to have fun. As you think back to the excitement you felt about riding, take some time to recognize how your current situation links back to that simple longing to be on a horse. Enjoyment is key. It's at the root of almost everyone's desire to ride. This book will show you how to support yourself in the adventure and joys of riding, wherever your journey may take you.

About the Book

After almost two decades as a mental skills coach, I am pleased to impart the gems I use most in my consulting practice to help clients enjoy riding horses and achieve success. My goal when writing this book was to keep it straightforward and accessible. I wanted to make the ideas constructive, engaging, and immediately relevant for your ride this afternoon, your lesson tomorrow, or your horse show next weekend.

The skills, qualities, and strategies presented in each chapter are designed to help all riders. Regardless of your discipline or ability level, you'll learn new ways to set goals, boost your confidence, and improve your focus, as well as to overcome the stress and fear when you ride or compete.

You will also discover how to maximize your potential with visualization techniques and to recover more quickly from a mistake. Plus, you'll find valuable tools for adjusting your energy as needed, maintaining a solution-oriented attitude, and communicating effectively with your team. And you will gather effective methods to help you prepare for any ride, as well as return from time away from the saddle with trust and composure.

Increasing your confidence and mental strength will further your enjoyment, goal achievement, and competitive success in your riding. The term "mental skills" will be used throughout the book to describe the psychological tools designed to enhance your thinking, approach, preparation, and partnering with your horse.

Insights from the Best

When you see riders at the Olympics maintain their composure while competing for a gold medal, have you ever wondered what they were thinking at that moment? Or how they got themselves prepared to focus and handle the amazing pressure they faced that day? Or wondered how they regrouped from a distraction or challenging circumstance?

The quotes on the pages ahead come from my interviews and conversations with top U.S. Olympic, international, and national riders and trainers about their psychological approach to being the best. Their honesty and openness was striking, as was their generosity of spirit in discussing their personal approach to riding, teaching, and competing. They shared their insights on psychological preparation and mental toughness, along with their methods for consistently achieving excellence.

Although competing in the Olympics may not be on your radar, you probably have goals and competitive objectives that are incredibly important to you. I hope these quotes will inspire you. Read them closely and you'll recognize some common themes among their approaches, such as an unflappable dedication to what works, a clear preparation routine on the day of a big class, and an amazing ability to focus under pressure. At the same time, each individual's psychological tactics are unique, and were developed over time in quite different ways.

Many of the riders and trainers told me that they had never had any formal exposure to sport psychology; some even said they didn't particularly believe in it! In spite of this, it's remarkable how closely their ideas, skills, and routines correspond to the information I present here. The main takeaway is this: No matter how you go about it, talk about it, or develop it, your psychological preparation and strength will play a significant role in your achievements. Period.

Dynamic, Personal Strategies

It took me many, many years of training to be an equestrian mental skills coach. Now, after earning my master's degree in sport psychology, having almost twenty years of experience consulting with individual riders, traveling across the country to give mental skills clinics to private barns and universities, as well as riding and showing myself, I am working with equestrians from a wide range of backgrounds, levels, and disciplines. But even after all this professional experience, is my personal preshow preparation routine completely serious, locked in, and unwavering? No. Do I encourage all riders to use a particular mental-skills routine all the time, no matter what? Not at all. These techniques should be anything but rigid.

As a personal example, some years ago I was getting ready to ride in the first round of a medal final. I was at the course board listening to my iPod when a friend walked up to me, noticed my headphones, and then motioned that she didn't want to interrupt. She was acquainted with the work I do and assumed I was doing some special part of my mental preparation. I took off one of my ear buds to let her listen. She started cracking up when she heard Kool and the Gang blasting, "Cel-e-brate good times, come on!"

She said, "I was expecting some visualization-type thing. Or some positive—what do you call those again—affirmations?"

Later on, I explained to her that my goals for that particular final were to go forward and ride by instinct (rather than getting too stuck on my plan), so I was experimenting with fun, energy-inspiring music. It was a valuable experience in that not only did it work, but it was yet another reminder to me of the importance of trusting your personal process.

In addition to "walking the talk," I'm also continually fascinated by my clients' creativity as we collaborate to develop their mental-preparation routines. We talk about how new ideas are essential for keeping things fresh and engaging to your mind. Some examples of their ingenuity: One client wears special perfume on show days that she associates with feeling calm and focused; another rider listens to the sound track from a movie that inspires him as he visualizes; and a third draws cartoons of her horse with captions of the positive statements she says to him to build trust and rapport. Will those techniques work for everyone? Probably not. But how fantastic and empowering that those riders believed in themselves enough to create their own strategies. You can do that too.

Building your mental toughness is a dynamic, personal process, and you are never done learning. Just as there is always more to learn about your horse, training methods, and horse care, there is always more to learn about yourself and what makes you tick. I hope the concepts here will inspire, help, and encourage you to be creative as you develop your own mental skills for riding. The best sport psychology practices are developed through a collaborative approach, and I'd like this book to serve as your invitation to begin.

1
Motivation

Identify Your Motivation and
Activate Your Skills

APPROACHING ANY ENDEAVOR (including riding a horse) with
a clear understanding of what motivates you is important.
It will help spark your enthusiasm in a powerful way. When you
can identify your motivation and call on it as needed, it's like having access to a special fuel that will propel you toward your goals.
Therefore, this is the best place to begin.

So ask yourself this basic question: What do I most enjoy about
my rides? Is it the wind whistling past your ears when you're out on
the trail for a gallop? Feeling harmony and grace with your horse
in the dressage arena? Experiencing a sense of calm confidence entering the show ring for your big jumper classic? The partnership
you feel when you're tacking your horse up, getting ready for your
Saturday morning lesson? We can experience joy with horses in so
many ways; it is a wonderful exercise to sit and appreciate them all.

Clearly identifying what you love about riding—your motivation—will help you in several respects:

- The choices you make about your training program and competition schedule will match your fundamental passion for riding, enabling you to put your best foot forward when creating goals and working toward them.

- By acknowledging special moments, positive emotions, the challenges of competing, and your eagerness for certain aspects of your training, you'll get reacquainted with your enjoyment of the sport.

- After a disappointing mistake or when you feel you have hit a training plateau, it can be difficult to stay positive. Reminding yourself of your passion for the sport and your desire to accomplish your goals can help you overcome a challenging time.

- When you're faced with a decision, such as choosing a horse to buy or a trainer to work with, choices that align with your core motivation will illuminate themselves and provide assistance in navigating your options.

In order to uncover your motivation, have access to all these benefits, and have an end result that you can easily access and use, I recommend developing a Motivation Statement.

I don't think I ever rode with the idea of being an Olympic athlete. I rode with the idea that riding was what fulfilled me, and riding better was what would fulfill me more.
                    —Michael Page, Olympic silver and bronze medalist,
                                        three-day eventing

Create a Motivation Statement

Take out a piece of paper and draw a circle in the middle of it. Write the name of your horse or "Riding" in the circle, and then sit and reflect on the following four questions:

1. What do you love about riding?

2. What type of rider would you like to be?

3. What positive feelings do you get when riding?

4. What are your best riding memories or experiences?

Allow about thirty to forty minutes for this brainstorming process, but take as long as necessary. As each answer comes up, write it down on a different line drawn from the circle outward—one answer per line. Some examples: *challenging myself, partnership with*

The brainstorming process for creating your Motivation Statement.

my horse, friends at the barn, feeling confident, excitement I feel before entering the show ring.

Be sure to include any positive reason you ride and don't give in to any temptations to edit yourself. You'll end up with what looks like a second-grade drawing of a sun, with the reasons you love to ride doodled all over the page. What fun!

> *I always had a passion for the sport and I always had a burning desire to want to do it . . . I don't know if that passion is something you can instill in somebody. I think it has to come from within. The same way you can have the most talented horse in the world, that has all the qualities and all the scope and all the carefulness, but if it doesn't have the heart and desire to want to be a good horse, you're not going to make it.*
>
> —Margie Engle, Olympic show jumping rider,
> ten-time AGA Rider of the Year

Next, step away from the process for a day or two. When you come back to it, circle the two or three items that seem to jump off the page at you. Then use your creativity to turn those top items into a short sentence, acronym, or motto—this will be your Motivation Statement. Remember, this needs to mean something only to you, and it's ideal to use powerful, precise language that makes you smile! For example, "Riding is challenging and exciting; every day I move one step closer to my goals." Or "Commitment + Confidence + Calm = C^3."

Here's what to do with your Motivation Statement:

- Write it on anything you can take with you, like sticky notes, index cards, or a bracelet. Put it on mirrors, in your trunk, on your boot bag, and any other place where you'll see it regularly.

It will be a dynamic reminder of your core motivation—this is your fuel, your fire.

- When you face problems achieving your goals, look at your Motivation Statement to help you stay determined and get back on track.

- Let others know your motivation so they can support you and help you appreciate your riding.

- See and feel your Motivation Statement happening in your mind every time you read it out loud or say it to yourself.

In the late '70s I started to want to be the best. It was my thing, to be the best. I started reading The Inner Game of Tennis . . . The Inner Game of Golf. *The psychology was being talked about more then. I'll never forget how it really helped me win the gold medal at the Pan Am Games—being able to focus, not being distracted by what was going on . . . visualization, and work I had done with [sport psychologist] Dr. Rotella.*
—Anne Kursinski, five-time Olympic show jumper, two-time Olympic silver medalist

Enjoy Your Ride

I hope you discover that fun is a large piece of what motivates you to ride. Of course, it's human nature to gravitate toward enjoyable activities. When you're new to something, it is often easy to feel happy through sheer participation. In addition, a fun activity often seems simple—not necessarily simple to master or perfect (many people enjoy feeling challenged and pushing past their limits), but simple in that you believe it will thrill you. The bonus is that when you have fun in the saddle, your mind and body can harmonize effortlessly with your horse—creating the ultimate riding experience.

But on the flip side, you can also come up against obstacles that hinder your riding pleasure. For example, it's hard to have fun when you're scared. Riding horses can create many different types of fear:

- Fear of falling

- Fear of failing

- Fear of going too fast

- Fear of getting hurt

- Fear of being embarrassed

The list goes on, and let's face it, riding these big animals can sometimes put you in situations that are just plain scary! It is also almost impossible to enjoy riding when you feel frustrated, defeated, or upset. If you get stuck in a rut, you may even forget what you enjoyed about riding in the first place. Could you use some help? Yes!

Examples of Motivation Statements

Positive + Attitude + Creates + Energy = P A C E

"We are team players who trust and inspire each other to do our best."

"I am excited to develop, excel, and achieve this year."

Best + Learning + Ultimate + Excellence = B L U E

"Every day we work together, we make progress and have fun."

A good mind is more valuable than intrinsic physical talent.
—Courtney King-Dye, Olympic dressage rider/trainer

Joanne, a dressage rider, came to me so afraid she couldn't do anything but walk her horse, Mattie. She'd had some bad experiences that had built up over time, leaving her anxious and only able to envision problems with her mare. When Joanne rode and felt consumed by fear, this was what she told herself:

- "I hate feeling so scared. It's embarrassing to be in the ring."

- "Mattie is just waiting to spook and bolt—I know she won't focus on me."

- "I feel so weak and loose that I'm sure to hit the ground today."

- "I don't deserve this horse."

We started our work together by identifying why she loved to ride. She brainstormed, wrote a Motivation Statement, and talked with me about everything she valued and appreciated in her relationship with her horse.

Joanne created this Motivation Statement: "We are focused, forward, and in harmony as a team." She refocused on what she loved about riding Mattie, and found courage and strength for her rides by using these statements:

- "I enjoy working together and creating an even rhythm."

- "I am focused on riding my plan."

- "We share positive energy and forward momentum."

- "I love humming a song that matches Mattie's steps."

It had been some time since Joanne had even thought about

the "good things" she felt when she rode, or reminded herself that she was making a choice each time she put her foot in the stirrup. By recognizing the positive aspects of riding her horse, and how they were more powerful than what she was afraid of, Joanne could move through her immobilizing fears and regain her confidence.

The above is an illustration of the philosophy that grounds this book and my sport psychology work with riders of all disciplines and abilities: Constantly move toward what you enjoy and want to create in your riding by adopting the mental skills to get you there. Whether you would like to go on a trail ride by yourself, build a relationship with a new horse, or win a ribbon at the Maclay Finals this year, the principles of mental strength and preparation are all the same.

> *There was a time about ten, eleven years ago that I didn't know*
> *if I wanted to ride anymore. I kept thinking that if I won this or*
> *won that, then I'd be happy. But it wasn't doing it . . . I took*
> *a break and went on some spirit journeys and retreats. That*
> *helped a lot with finding what's important to me. I ride now for*
> *the love of doing it. I'm not trying to prove anything.*
> —John French, three-time World Champion Hunter Rider,
>   U.S. show jumping team member

Let Curiosity Guide You

When I was in my early teens, I noticed a pattern at virtually every horse show I attended. I would start out the show on a Thursday or Friday feeling excited, but also butterfly-fiesta-in-my-stomach nervous and worried about pleasing my trainer, all of which created a lot of inconsistency in the ring. Frustrated and discouraged after looking forward to the show for days on end, I would try to regroup. Saturday would be a bit better, and by Sunday things would be really clocking along. I even went for a long, long stretch where I habitually won my last class on Sunday (often some sort of stake class in those days, which meant a little money). It was such a blast!

When someone would point out this phenomenon, usually my parents, it made me wonder why it happened. I also found that the more I acknowledged it, the greater my belief became that it would happen again. I would say to myself, "Oh, fun—it's Sunday. Good things are going to happen today!" I realized that because I rode and showed many different horses, the pattern couldn't be due to anything but me. I wondered, "Wait a second. Why can't I ride on Friday the same way I ride on Sunday? I'm the same person, with the same abilities—what's going on?" Although I had no answers then, my curiosity took root, and I never let go of the idea that one day I would figure it out.

Once I was in college, I discovered that psychology appealed to me most, especially the new application of the discipline called sport psychology. It seemed to me a perfect blend of my interest in sport and performance, particularly riding, and my desire to help people optimize how they thought, felt, and interacted with one another and the world.

As I considered how sport psychology principles could apply to my own experiences, I wondered if I could solve the mystery behind my trend of starting poorly and ending on such a high note at my horse shows. Ultimately, I did figure it out (thanks to many of the same techniques described in this book), and now I ride and show with valuable knowledge about how I work best, as well as a consistent mental-preparation routine.

Your curiosity is an important tool in guiding you toward skills and strategies that will help you be the best rider you can be. Take a moment now to answer these questions:

- What parts of your riding are you curious about? For example, have you noticed peaks and valleys in your ability that you would like to understand?

- What is the difference between the days you feel fantastic, brave, and effective, and the ones when you'd like to just disappear and not even finish your ride? What intrigues you about that phenomenon?

- What mental strengths do you feel you need?

- Where do you want to go with your riding? Is it having fun, being more confident, winning in the show ring, or staying focused while on your horse? (Maybe it's something completely different, or maybe you just said to yourself, "Hey, all of those sound great!")

When you dedicate yourself to figuring out the answers, you will tap into your motivation to understand your skills and improve on them. In other words, you will find your direction.

If I'm in Europe I watch my competitors. I watch the best. I learn from their mistakes and I learn from what they do really well. The minute you think you don't need to learn anymore, that's the minute you're going to go backward.

—Guenter Seidel, three-time Olympic
dressage bronze medalist

Access Your Abilities

Let's say your horse has a dynamic extended trot. It's a blast to ride and more exhilarating than anything you have ever done. However, if you're afraid to go big at a show and ask for that extension with confidence, it might as well not exist. You can have all the physical talents in the world, and so can your horse, but accessing them on cue is crucial to actualizing your potential. The following very different cases illustrate how mental strength provides the key to your physical skills, allowing you to ride in the direction of your goals.

Ruth, an older trail rider, came to me with a fear of her "naughty" horse, Rocket. It was springtime, she hadn't ridden to the beach since the previous year, and she wanted to go for a lope down by the water. To make that happen, Ruth believed she needed to build her overall confidence, because her horse had started testing her in a variety of situations. Although she had a good trainer she took lessons with occasionally, she was having a hard time on the trail by herself. Rocket would see ghosts in the bushes, decide his ability to turn left was on the fritz, stop dead as if obeying an invisible traffic light—all sorts of things to unnerve her, make her give up on the ride, and head for home.

We worked on Ruth's ability to focus on those elements in her control, which are the same for every rider and include the following:

- Positive expectations

- Body position

- Aids

- Energy

- Imagination

I reminded Ruth that she could access all of these during her ride to achieve her goals. She had forgotten how much she had at her disposal to solve any behavioral challenge Rocket could throw at her.

Out on a ride after Ruth and I had met several times, Rocket stopped at the very last section of trail before the beach. Ruth decided to take a breath, make him stand still, and wait until she could figure out how to outsmart him. In time, she turned and backed him down the slope to the beach, then turned forward once they were on the sand and proceeded to have a lovely lope next to the water as if nothing had happened. Reminding herself that she had control over her body, her decision-making, and her creativity allowed her to adopt a problem-solving attitude. She could stay calm and clear-headed in the moment, assured that she would find an answer.

In another case, very early in my career as a mental skills coach, a competitive and talented amateur-owner jumper rider named Linda came to me to work on why she hadn't had a win in a "big class." While she had been champion and reserve in her division, the Sunday class had always eluded her. Preparing for an upcoming jumper derby, we discovered that she frequently imagined negative outcomes when she visualized the important classes, and many of her images were a projection of her fear of failure. Because of this, she rarely visualized the whole class in its entirety.

After carefully retraining Linda in the finer details of visualization, including enhancing her ability to control every stride in her imagery, she went to her next show ready to prepare well and excel. At the show, Linda visualized the Sunday derby course in detail; she later told me that it rode exactly as she had imagined it. It turned out that she delivered the only clean round over a very trappy and technical course, resulting in her first "big win." The experience solidified her belief that physical talent was not enough; she knew she needed to have excellent mental skills to unlock her (and her horse's) physical ability in the show ring.

Clearly, it wasn't physical skills these riders were lacking, but *access to their capabilities.* Both riders learned that an improvement in their mental strength immediately allowed them to use their physical talents in a better way, and got them further down the road in the direction of their goals.

In '92 when I did the Olympic trials, it was strictly a whim. I mean there was no chance . . . I didn't even have a passport. I

hadn't ever left the country. I was riding a crazy thoroughbred
that nobody thought had any chance. I read this book by An-
thony Robbins, The Ultimate Power, which sort of helped me
feel confidence in a situation where I had none. I'd never been
at that level; I hadn't really competed around that group of people so I felt a little bit like an outcast. It helped me just to muster
up confidence within myself.

If I had gone in as the little fish in a big pond I think I'd
probably have performed that way. As a result, going in, OK, I
didn't walk in there like I owned the place—I definitely was still
feeling knots. But at the end when I made the team, which was
a shock to everybody, I just thought well, wow, that worked.

—Laura Kraut, three-time Olympic show jumper,
Olympic show jumping gold medalist

Laura Kraut on Cedric at the 2008 Olympic Games.

Head for Excellence

When I asked what direction you want to take your riding, you may
have quickly thought to yourself, "Direction? It's simple, I want to

Your Personal Tipping Point

McLain Ward, a two-time Olympic show jumping gold medalist, describes the awareness, motivation, focus, and immediate results he achieved when he first sought out sport psychology and began specific work on his mental skills.

"In [the spring of] 2008, I had had a terrible Palm Beach [circuit], in my opinion. I went to Tampa, and I had a time fault in the Grand Prix . . . At dinner that night I was a little bit upset . . . we actually sat at the dinner table for about four hours talking about it. There were comments [regarding how] some riders . . . thought that physically, I was one of the best, if not the best in the world, but mentally I 'didn't have a head' . . . and it bothered me. It really hit home."

McLain decided to see sport psychologist Dr. Rotella. He couldn't get in to see him, so he read one of his books, devouring it in three days. That was the year the hurricane hit during the Tampa Invitational, just as he went through his round.

"My focus never wavered. I had to exit the ring and wait fifty minutes to restart the course halfway through. It was a pretty decisive win in not very easy conditions. [They were] definitely conditions that before would have rattled me and frustrated me, and I probably would not have delivered the same performance.

I have to say I got in the car on Sunday morning to drive [home] with my wife and I said, 'I've got to meet this guy. I'm sold.' Like any new thing you incorporate [into your routine], there's a moment when (a) you need it and (b) it goes the right direction so you believe it . . . you can't halfway believe it. I believed it and I had an instant result."

be best." Whether you mean this in regard to competitive results ("I want to be *the* best") or your own personal progress and skill ("I want to be *my* best"), it is a good idea to set your GPS for "excellence"—not, please note, for the ever-elusive and troublesome mirage of "perfection." With excellence as your desired destination, you will hopefully be motivated to gather all available information, skills, and strategies to be successful.

As far as the psychological aspects of achieving excellence in sport, much research has been done in the area of peak performance, that time when you simultaneously maximize your mental and physical skills and far exceed your average level of performance. Not only have researchers identified which psychological characteristics you might typically experience when you're in the midst of a peak performance, but they have also looked at what types of mental preparation contribute to it. It's helpful to acquaint yourself with these factors as you build your mental toughness so you can recognize when you're truly doing well and identify which sport psychology skills could help you most. True peak performances are rare, but the quest for them is something that can reliably create excellence.

Here are some of the most common psychological reactions you may experience when riding at an excellent level or in the midst of a peak performance:

- Elevated self-confidence

- Feelings of control

- High energy

- Absence of fear (including no fear of failure)

- In-the-moment focus

- A sensation that you're on autopilot, exerting no effort

- Feeling like time has slowed down

Psychological skills and preparation often associated with creating peak performances and excellence in sport include the following:

- Using preparation plans

- Clear goals

- Enjoying the process, both preparation and performance

- Positive thinking, attitudes, and self-talk

- Physical readiness

- Personally optimal level of energy, both mental and physical

- Focus on current demands

- Upbeat communication with teammates

Many of these skills you may already have in place, while some you may only utilize from time to time, and still others you may want to build from the ground up. Regardless of where you stand now, it is helpful to be aware of these factors as you continue to draw your own map to success.

A TOP TIP

Just like a pony sneaking out of his stall to get the carrots
at the end of the barn aisle, we're all more effective
when our motivation drives our direction.

Chapter Highlights
Understand and Channel
Your Motivation

✔ Assess and utilize your motivation to ride with a Motivation Statement.

✔ Employ your curiosity to discover new keys to your success.

✔ Recognize the importance of using mental skills to access physical talent.

2
Confidence

Build Your Confidence by
Tracking Your Success

WHERE DOES YOUR confidence come from when you ride? What makes a horse so good at figuring out if you're confident or not? And why does it matter so much, particularly when you're in the saddle? Because your level of confidence about what you'd like to do with your horse (jump the scary roll top, stay connected through the downward transition, or walk through the big puddle) will determine whether you actually achieve it. It's just that simple. Not to mention, most of your best overall rides and most enjoyable riding moments happen when you're feeling confident and competent.

Now I can hear you saying, "Great, but I can't just create confidence out of thin air or buy it at the tack shop." Good point! So let's examine some straightforward ways to boost your confidence;

they all revolve around having methods to track your progress and growth as a rider.

Goal Setting

Some time ago, during one of my mental skills clinics, we started talking about setting goals. A small, slender woman in the group immediately crossed her arms and scooted her chair backward. "I don't believe in writing down goals," she said with a frown. "They only stress me out. They just remind me of things I don't do well. In fact, I get frustrated just thinking about them because they seem so far away. Is it OK if I just sit this part out?" Although everyone else was a bit taken aback at first, what ensued was a lively, productive discussion that cleared up a lot of the participants' misunderstandings about goals.

Contrary to what many people believe, goal setting is actually about identifying where and how you are making progress, not continually focusing on what you don't yet know or have. *Setting goals for improving your riding skills and giving yourself credit for both effort and progress builds confidence in a way nothing else can.*

To be sure, you have probably read about the importance of goal setting in horse training books, magazines, self-help books—the list is long. Maybe you have some experience with the process. Do you set goals in a systematic way? Do you have a method for refreshing, recording, and adjusting them? Do you believe in their usefulness? If so, great! If not, please keep an open mind—you may be surprised at how easy they are to integrate into your riding routine.

Often riders understand that goals are a good idea, but they don't know how to make them useful in their day-to-day riding and showing. So they ignore their goals or write them down and shove them into a drawer, or think about them as a pass/fail exam that creates more stress and anxiety. My purpose here is to reset your belief and investment in the goal-setting process. The following section will go over the basics and make clear links between goals and improving your confidence on your horse.

> *Goal setting is something that is natural for me, but its importance became starkly clear when a sponsor asked me to write down my five-year goals for him. This was before the Olympics and before I had any top Grand Prix horses. I wrote to have two Grand Prix horses competing internationally and have a few very young horses to bring along. Two years later I had Myth and Idy, and three three-year-olds, and [that sponsor] didn't buy them.*
>
> —Courtney King-Dye, Olympic dressage rider/trainer

Courtney King-Dye on Mythilus at the 2008 Olympic Games.

GOAL-SETTING BASICS

We learn better when information is presented in real terms rather than in the abstract. If you make something personally relevant, you will care more, learn more, and benefit more from the process. To that end, please get a nice piece of paper or pad and your favorite pen. Write some goals you are currently working toward in your riding while you peruse the following nine goal basics (be sure to adapt and edit as you go):

1. **Emphasize performance goals (balance outcome goals as needed).** A performance goal is based on your own progress, while an outcome goal is measured by the results of a competition. Emphasize performance goals; focus on achieving your personal best and trust that great outcomes will follow. If you compete, you may naturally have outcome goals that anchor your motivation and effort, but balance those with performance objectives that are within your control.

    Here is an example of each type:

    - *Performance goal:* Stay straight into each corner to get clean lead changes on course.

    - *Outcome goal:* Finish in the top ten of my division this year.

2. **Let information from your trainer help you create and prioritize your performance goals.** Choose your goals from what you have been hearing from your trainer in your recent lessons or at horse shows. Maybe you have been working on keeping your fingers closed on the reins, or remembering to lift your chin by thinking "tall" during your rides. Either trust yourself to choose the top three goals to focus on for the next month, or ask your trainer for advice about what to put at the top of your list.

3. **Set challenging, realistic goals.** Your goal should stretch you, but be something you feel is truly possible. If you don't know if it is realistic, ask someone you trust for help—such as your trainer, a clinician who knows you well, or a riding friend. A challenging, yet realistic goal for a beginning dressage rider might be to learn to sit the trot for five minutes.

   I think for goal setting to build confidence, your goals have to be realistic and attainable.
   —Courtney King-Dye, Olympic dressage rider/trainer

4. **Phrase your goals positively.** Your mind and body process positive action words more rapidly and effectively than negative ones like "don't," "stop," or "never." Instead of "Stop looking down," phrase the same goal as "Keep my eyes up on a focal point."

5. **Write down your goals.** Recording your objectives will help crystallize them. Be clear and succinct. This process ensures that reviewing, adjusting, and updating can happen easily.

6. **Use powerful language to activate your imagination.** "Build a forward, active canter in my opening circle." Or "Create poise by stretching tall and opening my chest before I enter the ring at the show."

7. **Build a clear relationship between short- and long-term goals.** Think about a long-term goal and build backward from it to ensure that your goals support each other. Long-term goal: Move up to preliminary by the end of this year. Short-term goal: Use leg and get to the middle of every jump while running cross-country in my next two events.

We always have a meeting where we talk about short-term goals and long-term goals. It helps me plan the rider's career [and decide] when to stretch them and why I would want to stretch them. I believe when they've accomplished a goal it's good for their confidence.

—Stacia Madden, top hunter/jumper/equitation trainer

8. **Focus on just two to three short-term goals at a time.** By selecting a small number of goals to concentrate on, they'll be easier to bring into the ring with you. Because your mind can handle only so much at once, keeping your goals clear and succinct will allow you to effectively integrate them into your ride, test, or course plan.

9. **Track your goals monthly and adjust as necessary.** Recording, adjusting, and updating your goals is helpful and essential. It reinforces the fact that goals are fluid, and interacting with them regularly is more important than adopting a simple pass/fail attitude. This will also protect you from feeling defeated and negative regarding the goal-setting process when things don't turn out as planned.

GOAL STRATEGIES ARE CRUCIAL

Each goal is only as valuable as the strategies you devise to support it. For example, let's say you are an equitation rider who wants to have a 30 percent stronger lower leg before an important show next month. However, without a clear plan for making that happen, it's doubtful you will achieve that goal anytime soon. Therefore, write specific, action-oriented strategies for turning every goal into a reality. They should include both mental and physical ideas. Take a look at this example:

Performance goal: Strengthen my lower leg by 30 percent.

1. Ride without irons for a minimum of ten minutes every day.

2. Run for twenty to thirty minutes three times a week.

3. Choose two places in my ring to say "Heels" to myself, then each time I ride past that place on the flat, step into my heel and lengthen my leg.

Need more physical strategies? Brainstorm with books, your trainer's help, past exercises from clinics you have attended, training videos, or riding friends you respect. Need more mental strategies to support your goals? This book is full of mental tools and techniques that are ideal for using as strategies. As you read on, be sure to add ideas that support your goals.

INCORPORATE GOALS INTO YOUR RIDES

Whether you're riding your horse on your own, doing an exercise in a lesson, or riding a course or test at a show, including your performance goals in each ride is vital. In this way, they are never ends unto themselves, sitting in isolation on your desk. They are an active part of your day-to-day riding and competing that directs your focus and helps you create success in the ring.

Imagine a dressage rider facing her first show at Second Level, Test 1. Her first task is to memorize the test itself, where and when the transitions and movements occur—the "what." Integrating her performance goals into her ride helps create the "how"—creating some of the details for how she plans to ride the test to the best of her ability. For example, her performance goal to keep her upper body tall is integrated into her test by planning to stretch up before every upward or downward transition; in fact, her ride plan should include two to three performance goals throughout the test. Add in the "how's" (your performance goals) to your ride plan, and you will feel the "what" (the ride itself) improve exponentially.

Post-Ride Notes

So you have a terrific set of goals in place and you are building them into your rides. Then it happens—the amazing, fantastic, wonderful ride. Have you ever had this occur at a show and found yourself finishing the ride/test/run/course in a bit of shock? "How did that happen? Can I do it again tomorrow? Why were we so good?" These are but a few of the questions that may have buzzed through your head as you accepted congratulations from your trainer and friends. It may have felt like lightning struck, but it is important to remember that you had a major part in creating the success.

Reflecting on how the goals you focused on within the ride translated into success is one of the very best ways to build belief in yourself as a rider (*Note:* On some days, success may come only in small pieces; it is important to collect and polish those gems in every ride, even when there are bigger mistakes within the ride that catch your attention first!).

Take time to write down post-ride reflections.

Certain equestrian disciplines lend themselves to reflecting on rides by keeping logs and riding journals, and there are personality types more drawn to this kind of process. Have you ever written notes after your rides? What did you keep track of? It is important to note that all logs or journals are not created equal. To take advantage of

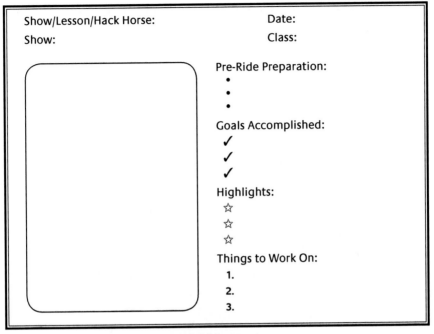

Show/Lesson/Hack Horse: Date:
Show: Class:

Pre-Ride Preparation:
•
•
•

Goals Accomplished:
✓
✓
✓

Highlights:
☆
☆
☆

Things to Work On:
1.
2.
3.

Post-Ride Notes

all the benefits of tracking your rides, it's helpful to use a method or template to guide you and help you focus on your achievements.

For example, here's a well-written goal and a post-ride reflection:

- *Goal:* Improve seat at the canter by relaxing my lower back and thighs.

- *Post-ride reflection:* Today the canter work at the end of the lesson felt balanced and connected; I really concentrated on releasing the tension and fatigue in my back.

Post-Ride Notes are a valuable template to use when briefly recording a ride, test, schooling session, round, or class (see the illustration above). They are designed to help you record the following:

1. Details: Day, horse, location, type of ride.

2. **Pre-ride preparation:** Things you did before you got on your horse that helped you get ready for the ride, such as listening to upbeat music on your iPod; eating a banana; parking your car at the barn and spending a minute taking some Circle Breaths before you got out and went to tack up; walking around the show ring to orient yourself to the course, jumps, and environment.

When I had success, why did I have success? Looking back after the fact [and asking], "Why was it like that?" . . . Preparation, how you sleep, what you eat . . . little things like that. Being conscious of it. You're an athlete, you've got to treat yourself as an athlete.

—Anne Kursinski, five-time Olympic show jumper,
two-time Olympic silver medalist

3. **Goals accomplished:** Goals achieved, either in full or in part, during that ride. These were goals already in place before the lesson or ride, or things you (or your trainer) identified during

Anne Kursinski on Great Point.

the ride to be goals for that day. Some examples: used focal points at the ends of the ring to stay straight after your lines; exhaled before downward transitions, visualized each exercise before getting started.

4. **Highlights:** Moments during your ride you felt proud of or enjoyed, compliments you received from others—basically, times the clouds parted, the sun came out, the birds sang and you said to yourself, "This is why I ride."

Don't train every day with only one goal in mind because you're going to be very disappointed if something falls apart. You have to look at the big picture. Enjoy the training part . . . enjoy the process . . . enjoy the work with the horse.

—Guenter Seidel, three-time Olympic
dressage bronze medalist

5. **Things to work on:** Ideas for solving challenges or fixing the mistakes that happened during the ride. Let's say you had a sloppy upward transition because the tractor distracted your horse, so your item to work on might be "Wake up our connection with my leg before I ask for a transition." This may have been a solution you or your trainer came up with during the ride, or something that occurs to you as you sit and write your notes—either way, you are writing only the solution to the situation (not a description of the problem and the negative emotions associated with it).

6. **In the ring:** Diagrams or small drawings of exercises you rode during the lesson, such as courses, movements, tests, flatwork, and cross-country segments. As you recall them, you'll be accessing your muscle memory and strengthening the positive memories.

Not only is the process of writing Post-Ride Notes incredibly valuable, but the product they become is also a significant resource. In fact, once you have a collection of notes, they become like a small database of confidence, inspiration, and capabilities. Let's say you have a month's worth of completed Post-Ride Notes. They are now useful in a variety of ways:

- Review them before a lesson, clinic, or competition to build confidence.

- Remind yourself of your abilities after a challenging experience.

- They can help you get back into the swing of things after time away from riding.

- Look at them for inspiration for exercises to design and ride on your own when hacking or schooling by yourself.

"Two Positives" Rule Examples

"I counted in every corner and that helped our rhythm stay the same."

"I kept looking ahead even when she tried to spook at the garbage truck."

"I used my leg first for every half-halt."

"We stayed comfortable all the way around; the gallop felt smooth and consistent."

"Each time I had a thought about winning, I said to myself, 'Just ride the plan.'"

"The tempis were terrific because I kept breathing."

The "Two Positives" Rule

Eden, a junior hunter rider, would come out of the ring crying whenever she made a noticeable mistake on course, and her mom was questioning if she should continue to let her compete. The pattern was wearing on the trainer who couldn't figure out how to get through to her, the emotional roller coaster was eroding the girl's confidence, and the whole process was so exhausting that her mom started dreading going to the horse shows. As a last ditch effort, the mom sent Eden to work with me to see if we could give her some tools to deal with what had developed into quite a difficult situation.

It turned out that Eden was so focused on pleasing others (namely, her trainer and parents) that she was putting an inordinate amount of pressure on herself. When she made a mistake, she felt like a "bad" rider, unworthy of her horse and her trainer's time. Eden stopped being able to trust herself to make the right decisions in the ring. With each mistake, she lost more confidence, and she felt emotionally devastated with alarming regularity at horse shows.

Once we established a solid working relationship, Eden agreed to commit to the "Two Positives" Rule as a way of countering the devastating pattern. When you are a devotee of this rule, you agree to say (either quietly to yourself or out loud to your trainer, a friend, or possibly your horse) two specific things you liked about your exercise/course/test/ride and why—this is done before anything else is said, if possible. Your goal is to name something big or small within that experience that was well done and a specific way you helped bring it about.

This was very difficult for Eden to do and required a lot of patience—mostly her being patient with herself and sticking with it until it was an easier and more comfortable process. Coming out of the ring after a junior hunter round where she was very deep to the single oxer and quite disappointed, for example, she would take a breath and first say something like, "I really kept my elbow relaxed and rode up to the first jump well, and I remembered to use my voice in the two-stride to help him relax." Once she had built this routine as a habit, it truly helped smooth out her roller coaster of confidence while deepening her awareness that every ride contained some things to be proud of and enjoy. Another benefit that occurred over time was that she started to begin each ride wondering about and looking for her "two positives," thus expecting—and creating—wonderful successes.

The "Two Positives" Rule will be a big help in maintaining your foundation of confidence. You are not ignoring that there are always things to work on and improve, but emphasizing the importance of supporting yourself and acknowledging that your skills create some successes in every single ride. Although it may be difficult at first, persevere and this can become a habit that contributes to your steady progress as a rider.

> *I think another important thing we have to learn is that we don't win often. This is what I do with my students, in any round—good, bad, indifferent—I always try to find the good points . . . Your win ratio in the jumpers, particularly at the higher level, is low. You have to take away something that keeps you feeling good about yourself when you're sixth.*
>
> —Laura Kraut, three-time Olympic show jumper,
> Olympic show jumping gold medalist

Watching Videos for Reinforcement

When was the last time you saw a video of yourself riding? This is a simple way to give yourself feedback, watch your progress in action, and chronicle your accomplishments. Video is much easier to come by today than it was in the past, since many cameras and phones are equipped with video components.

Use these four video goals to aid you in building your overall confidence:

1. Get video of yourself in a lesson or show one to three times a month. Strategize ahead of time and figure out who can record you—possibly a family member, friend, observer, or groom. You may be able to easily trade with a barn buddy; then set up the process as a regular occurrence rather than a once-in-a-blue-moon event.

2. Watch your video by yourself with an eye for what you are accomplishing. Enjoy reliving the ride; remember your feelings of fun and satisfaction during the highlights that stand out to you.

3. After watching it once to take everything in, watch it again and select specific things you're happy to see, such as highlights (a great canter transition); moments where you accomplished a

Watch videos of yourself to boost your confidence.

performance goal (like keeping your eye up on the landing side of a jump); or skills and talents you are becoming more aware of (hey, your leg is actually very quiet at the sitting trot!).

Pause the video often to give yourself time to absorb what you're seeing. It can also be valuable to write down the positive things and date them so you can further cement their existence.

4. Watch sections that include mistakes or challenges only once or twice, and then pause the tape to brainstorm and imagine solutions to the situation. As you utilize what your trainer said that day, or would have said, to help you solve the situation, also think of things you have done in the past that helped. Then visualize yourself riding the same section again, enacting the solution, and finishing the section with a positive result.

I think video is very good. It's a great teaching aid. People think they look like one thing and they really don't at all . . . [They can] see their mistakes and/or realize they look way better than they think they do.
—Anne Kursinski, five-time Olympic show jumper,
two-time Olympic silver medalist

A TOP TIP

Confidence is like a bank account:
It's best to make regular deposits and watch
your balance grow.

Chapter Highlights
Skills to Build Confidence

✔ Set quality goals.

✔ Create strategies for each goal.

✔ Integrate performance goals into your rides.

✔ Use the "Two Positives" Rule.

✔ Watch videos to identify your progress.

3

Focus

Staying in the Moment

W HEN WAS THE last time you were on your horse and your mind was somewhere else? Yesterday, you say? Oh, dear! Were you looking down the road, anticipating the garbage truck that could spook your horse again? Or were you noticing the gusts of wind and worrying about the small dust tornadoes that might blind you? Perhaps you found yourself getting tense as you imagined jumping the newly painted black panel jump—even though you were only just starting to warm up? During these moments, your horse was pretending to participate, your trainer was shaking her head, and you felt slightly disconnected mentally and physically but didn't know what to do about it.

Now recall an opposite experience, a time when you were beautifully in sync with your horse and the movements you were performing together. Your focus was effortlessly in the moment, and you felt energized and strong as you made subtle adjustments and rode your horse beautifully. Well, guess what? This type of experience can happen more than you think when you have the right tools to harness your attention and direct your focus. As we explore some of the best ones here, look for ways to fold them into your riding routine, both at home and at shows.

Staying in the Moment

Mary was a young equitation rider who always worried about what others would think of her round; she was absolutely mortified when she made a mistake. One day she came out of the show ring frustrated and upset (again), and her trainer told her to get off her horse.

"Mary, we have to do something about this! You let one small mistake ruin your focus and send you off the deep end. You let little mistakes snowball into much bigger problems because you're so worried about what other people will think about your round. So here is what you are going to do right now: I want you to walk around the ring and ask every person you run into what he or she thought of your trip and how you could have ridden better. Go on. Start with her right over there." Although Mary was beyond terrified, her trainer was not a person to ignore, so she took off her gloves, twisted them into a knot, and walked over to the woman watching on the rail.

"Ah, excuse me. Um, my trainer, well, I was wondering if you could please tell me what you thought of my round and, um, if you have suggestions. I just went on that grey horse over there." Mary's face was bright red and she stood looking at the ground, awaiting a colorful description of the small but escalating mistakes she had made in the ring.

"Oh honey, I'm so sorry. I don't think I saw your trip; I was waiting for my friend to get here. Lovely horse—did you do well?" Mary mumbled a "Fine, thank you," and walked away relieved.

The next two girls standing ringside were acquaintances of Mary's, and they giggled as they showed her the texts they had been sending to their friend in Hawaii as they stood at the ring "watching." On and on it went, and Mary started to feel a weight lifting as she talked to people. She slowly figured out that either people hadn't seen her round or if they had, they'd already forgotten about it. What a valuable lesson! From that day forward, Mary knew she had better stay focused on her round while she was in the ring because aside from her trainer and a friend or two, no one else was. She made it her new priority to *stay in the moment*.

Being focused *is* staying in the moment—whether you're listening to your trainer tell you a flatwork exercise, riding four-tempis in your dressage test, finding the line to the trakehner on your course walk, or cantering to the first jump at medal finals—you are completely aware of what you're doing, thinking, and feeling. Staying in the moment while riding is what allows you to effectively react and respond to your horse, the plan, and the environment. You can then trust your instincts, access all your best mental and physical skills, and create the best ride you are capable of on that day.

Shortly after Mary's epiphany about the importance of staying in the moment, she and her mom thought it would be a good idea if she consulted with me on a regular basis. We continued to build her awareness of things that enhanced or derailed her focus in the ring. Although she had truly moved past her distractibility regarding the audience's opinion of her ride, she still struggled with her tendency to "think behind herself" when she or her horse made a mistake.

On the plus side, Mary realized that as she walked into the show ring, she needed to look directly ahead of her, narrowing her focus to where she wanted to go and shutting herself off from distractions (such as people at the gate and the rider exiting the ring.). Understanding both her challenges and best strategies for her focus was a critical starting point, and something for you to figure out for yourself.

What typically derails your focus?

- When do you find yourself out of sync with what is happening underneath you?

- When does your focus become too internal (with a hyper-awareness on your thoughts, judgments about the ride, feelings, or physical sensations), taking you away from effectively riding and reacting in the moment?

- When do you "go blank" and forget the details of what you're supposed to be doing?

- What triggers your tendency to think too far ahead or too far behind yourself in the middle of a ride?

What enhances your focus?

- What do you do before you get on your horse to gather yourself together mentally for your ride?

- During a school, lesson, or ride at a show, when do you find yourself most focused? Why?

- How do you recover from a distraction during a ride?

When you're selecting strategies for staying in the moment, it's useful to start with a thorough understanding of what hurts as well as helps your concentration. Assessing your focus may be challenging; if you need support, try to come at it from a variety of angles. A few suggestions: Watch video of recent past rides to remember what you were thinking and when; ask your trainer what habits he or she observes with respect to your focus; write Post-Ride Notes (see page 26) to reflect on the ebb and flow of your attention during a ride. Enhancing your awareness will help you recognize and strengthen your good habits as well as select the appropriate tools to face your challenges.

In and Out of Control

Getting dressed for your afternoon class at the horse show, you begin to notice the weather forecast's promised dark clouds rolling in toward the barns. You've been worrying all day about the weather, because you have had bad rides when an unsettled atmosphere made you and your horse tense.

"Ugh," you think to yourself, "I hope the rain doesn't start right when I get on. The horses are all going to be wild in the warm-up ring—this could be a disaster." On and on your thinking circles, dragging your focus away from the good preparation and quality ride you had been planning. You have fallen into the most basic focus trap—spending too much time and energy on something that is ultimately out of your control.

When you picked up this book, chances are you were looking for things to do, think, and practice that could bolster your mental strength for riding. Well, you have reached one of the most critical points about the mental strength necessary for riding a horse well: to be aware of what is and is *not* in your control, and to always direct your attention and energy wisely. Is worrying about the storm going to help you stay positive, focused, and strong?

The weather is just one of many things out of our control.

Can't Control the Weather

How you react to situations out of your control is key to your success. Olympic show jumper Margie Engle shares an experience at Spruce Meadows that depicts how her attitude and concentration helped her excel in less-than-ideal conditions.

"I remember one time at Spruce Meadows I was anchor of the team. I had to go either clear or four [faults] for us to win the Nations Cup . . . And the weather is always changing there. I remember that right about as I was getting ready to go in the ring, it literally started to hail the size of golf balls. It was hitting poor Perin in the head.

"It was just amazing. I've never in my life seen hail that big. It was so big it actually stayed on the ground. It almost looked like snow. It was just literally hitting him. He was so tough.

"But you just try and look at things in a positive way as much as you can. The more you can look at things in a positive light the better. It doesn't help to be negative. [I didn't want to think], 'I have to be tentative. He's going to be scared of the water because the hail is splashing and he's going to be worried about the hail hitting him in the face and get backed off.' You just have to ride through it.

"So I remember [the hail] hitting the water jump, splashing. I just thought, 'Well, that's an advantage for me.' Sometimes after [horses] get older and jump the water enough times, they get a little complacent, and I thought, 'Well, maybe—and I'm just trying to look at things in a positive way—maybe that splashing will make him try harder.' And he did. He jumped it great. It was almost like as scary as it was, [it helped him] jump it even better than normal and he ended up pulling through a clear round."

No. Of course awareness of your surroundings is important (safety being a priority of good horsemanship), but only as it helps you make smart choices about how to handle the situation competently.

I'll say to myself, "There's no sense getting nervous, because you have no control over the future really. You can only control the present, the ride." So it's a waste of time worrying about that. Because it will all come down to being in the present.
—John French, three-time World Champion Hunter Rider,
U.S. show jumping team member

Brainstorming a list of things in and out of your control in riding is crucial to building your day-to-day awareness of how you're directing your attention. After all, how can you adjust your thinking if you are unaware of what you're thinking about? Also, you probably have habits that have made you feel like you aren't in control—such as your position, energy level, or self-talk—that you *most certainly do* have control over.

This exercise is one of the most effective ways to become more aware of where you direct your focus and attention in a typical day's riding.

To begin, take out a nice piece of paper, pad, or journal and brainstorm a list of everything that is *out of your control*. Make a column on the left side of the paper and include these examples:

- Weather

- Your trainer's lesson plan

- The judge

- Your competitors

- Horse's mood and performance

- Outside-the-ring distractions

- How others communicate with you

- The past

What else can you think of?

There are many, many things to add to this list! In addition, before you start to refute any of these that you think are in your control, remember that there is much in riding we *influence*, but do not ultimately control, such as a judge's opinion of us or of our horse, or our horse's execution of the requested movements. Be thoughtful and thorough as you round out this list; it will help you recognize when you are getting stuck, distracted, or worried about something you cannot completely control (instead of shifting gears and crafting a workable solution to the situation).

Now, on the other side of the paper, brainstorm and jot down a list of all the things *in your control* when you ride. Here are some examples:

- Physical performance/position/use of aids

- Energy level

- Preparation (including nutrition/hydration, rest, organization, fitness level, and time management)

- How you communicate with others

- Reaction and response to things out of your control

- Horse's preparation

- Your goals and expectations

- Focus (including ride or course plan, vision, and peripheral awareness)

Although these are some of the main ones, you will definitely find more as you think about it. *The importance of directing your focus to things that are in your direct control is at the heart of your success as a rider, competitor, and athlete.* It is one of the simplest differences between an average-thinking rider and a consistently excellent rider whose focus is rock solid. The latter rider—the one with the spot-on focus—may have also been showing in the afternoon when the rainstorm was rolling in. However, that rider was reminding herself to . . .

1. Be on a little early, in case her horse needed a few extra laps of canter work before settling down into their warm-up routine (horse preparation)

2. Take some extra long, slow breaths as she finished getting ready and getting on in order to calm the butterflies starting to riot in her stomach (energy level)

3. Think about things that were important when riding in the rain—such as keeping her fingers closed, getting down in her heel in every corner, and using her voice to keep her horse's attention (reaction and response)

Spend the next couple of weeks noticing when and where you get stuck thinking about the factors out of your control in your riding. Make a conscious choice to change your thought pattern by addressing the issue with something that is within your control, and then give yourself a pat on the back as you notice the boost to your confidence.

I'm always talking to the riders to make sure they're making good decisions with the variables they have control over. I talk a lot about being on time and feeling organized. I don't allow the

*kids to get undressed between classes unless there's a long delay
because I feel like it leads to disorganization. I'm really big on
the issues that we have control over . . . making sure we make
good decisions with [those things] so that the things we don't
have control over are easier to tolerate.*

    —Stacia Madden, top hunter/jumper/equitation trainer

Cue Words

Beth, an amateur jumper rider who had started riding as an adult,
came to me to get help with her focus in the ring. Extremely driven
in her job, she was using that same tenacity and determination to
work her way up the jumper ranks. While this approach was useful,
it was also getting a bit unwieldy. Beth took copious notes after each
lesson and had lists upon lists of things she needed to work on and
accomplish. Instead of making her more focused during her rides,
this process was causing her to feel increasingly scattered and distracted because she was worried about doing everything, all at once.

    To boost her focus and attention, Beth worked on prioritizing
her goals (with the help of her trainer), and we came up with some
shortened, powerful reminders for her to use in the ring. These are
called "cue words"—simple, powerful words that help direct your
focus and trigger a particular response. For example, she needed to
look earlier in the corners, particularly in jump-offs, so she made
a cue word of "Look." Beth also needed to be more determined in
her rounds, so "Commit" was her cue to come forward out of turns,
believe in her decision, and trust in her horse. As illustrated here,
it is important to note that cue words can trigger a specific action
by (1) becoming the shorthand version of a performance goal, or
(2) encapsulating a motivational or emotional component that is
important to the ride.

Cue Words and Performance Goals

Cue words are a way to turn your goals into action-oriented hooks for your focus. Say your trainer has been having you work on the quality of your upward transitions. He wants you to stretch up, activate your leg, and keep your eye up on a specific target so your horse understands where to direct the new forward momentum. You—being the smart, proactive rider that you are—take it upon yourself to set this performance goal: "Crisp transitions: Use an active leg to create forward energy toward the target."

To help you remember this goal within your rides, you next choose a cue word to use that encapsulates the goal, such as "Active." During your rides (either in a lesson or when hacking on your

More Tools for Improving Your Focus

Sport psychology is designed to help athletes think more effectively. (Never forget that riders are athletes too.) So it's no surprise that many strategies have a variety of benefits—including improved focus and concentration. Please be on the lookout for these additional focus-enhancing tools throughout the book:

- Setting performance goals

- Visualization

- Centering

- Pre-ride routines

- Energy management techniques

own), you say "Active" to yourself as you prepare for each upward transition. This triggers an instantaneous response of stretching and activating your leg, and finding a specific target for your eye. Your improved focus has helped you be successful on a skill you have been working to improve (by the way, your trainer is thrilled to see steady improvement in your upward transitions even on the days he is having you attend to other priorities).

CUE WORDS AND MOTIVATION OR EMOTION

Cue words can also be designed to create a feeling or energy level you are hoping to bring to an aspect of your riding. After the bell rings, a dressage rider looking to create a brilliant, forward ride at championships may say the cue word "Free" as part of the mental routine she goes through prior to entering the arena. This word sums up her desire to ask for everything she can, allow her horse to be expressive and forward, and enjoy the performance.

Checkpoints

"I came out of the ring and realized that I went blank during my class. I didn't remember to do any of my goals."

"I thought I was lifting my hands, but when I looked at the video, they were below his withers!"

"How can I stay focused on the quality details during my test? It goes by in such a blur."

"I am so busy evaluating what just happened over the last jump, it's a wonder I can remember where I am going half the time!"

If any of these statements sound even vaguely familiar, learning to use checkpoints during your rides will help you harness your focus more effectively. Checkpoints maintain your focus on a behavior or goal that directly contributes to your success within a particular part of your exercise, course, or test. To create a checkpoint, you "flag" a particular place (or places) within an exercise to remind you to execute a skill. For example, if you're working on keeping your reins short and lifting your hands (a performance goal you set for yourself), but are having trouble remembering to do so during your rides, try this:

1. Create checkpoints at places within your ride by using land-marks in the ring (say, the in-gate and the big tree at the top of the ring) or at places you determine ahead of time that will occur within a course/test/class (for example, at the top of the hill before heading down the slope into the water).

2. As you ride by or through the checkpoint, use a cue word such as "Lift" to remember to close your fingers around the reins and lift your hand up and in front of your body.

You can see the progression from performance goal (keep your reins short and lift your hands) to cue word ("Lift") to integration within your ride (two checkpoints in the ring to use anytime you are hacking or lessoning in your ring at home).

If something unpleasant pops into my head I send it away. I think, OK, no, don't go there. . . If I start to have doubt or I start to question myself, I stop it immediately and I say, "No, no, just go back, focus on the job. Pay attention to the good parts and how it's going to go well." You can't ignore that there are tests out there. The whole course is a test. You might fail a part of it and that's a reality. But I try not to focus on the fail-ing; I try to focus on how I'm going to succeed and really stay-ing calm.

—Laura Kraut, three-time Olympic show jumper,
Olympic show jumping gold medalist

Ride Plans

Without a quality ride plan, just about anything can happen during an exercise, course, or test. You may indeed have picked up the right lead canter at "E," jumped the diagonal line in six strides, or made it out of the water and up the big bank—but there may have been a few too many "Mrs. Toad's Wild Ride" elements present. Although those moments can happen even with an excellent ride plan in place, the odds are certainly more in your favor that you will execute a smooth, stylish ride when you have assessed and analyzed the best way to get it done ahead of time.

Bernie Traurig (right) and George Morris walking the course.

Putting the puzzle together piece by piece comes from your prep-
aration, course walk, visualization—all of that builds the plan.
Then when you're in the air over each jump, you know exactly
what's coming up and exactly what to do the moment you hit
the ground.
　　—Bernie Traurig, rider, clinician, and Founder/President,
Equestriancoach.com

You and your trainer may create the bulk of your ride plan together, but you also need to fill in the plan with the strategies you
have been working on in your training and the specific ways you
will direct your focus.

To accomplish this, integrate performance goals (and cue words)
into a test or course so that as you memorize and learn the requirements of the ride, you can combine them with details of how you
will do them well, thus creating a complete focus plan for the whole
performance.

"Get out to the edge of the tree line on your right—that will give
you the best track to the chevron," says your trainer as you walk the
cross-country course. You make a note on your map and continue
on your merry way, excited to be walking your first Preliminary out-
ing. Then as you sit down later that day to make the course plan
for your cross-country run, you think through how to execute the
subtleties you and your trainer have discussed.

Let's look at an example: You need to get out to the tree line
before that chevron, which means as you round the turn, you have
to put all your knowledge, trainer's teachings, and jump schools into
action. You decide that your focus for that section needs to progress
something like this:

1. Lock your eye into your focal point.

2. Stretch up.

3. Add a half-halt.

4. Activate your inside leg to leg and outside rein to maintain the line to the jump.

Thinking through that progression, then imagining (and more importantly *feeling*) that sequence when you visualize the whole course will be the difference between hoping for a positive result and training your focus to be spot-on when you come galloping through the turn.

Building a complete ride plan helps you teach your mind and body the ways you will create a quality ride. You may not control the test or course, but you have control over how you plan and respond to the questions posed. The plan will also help you stay engaged in the moment so you can go to a Plan B as needed (having a terrific plan does not guarantee it will all unfold as you imagine, of course). Starting with a well-crafted plan will enable you to ride mindfully and smoothly, no matter what adjustments you may need to make in the moment.

Leslie Howard on Priobert.

It's just a matter of walking your course, having your plan and then going in the ring and executing it. The only thing mentally that I would add that has helped me is that I'm very tunnel vision. No matter what I'm doing in life, whether I'm teaching or riding or especially competing in the ring, I really am very tunnel vision. It never occurs to me to think who's standing on the side of the rail or if there's one person in the stands or fifty thousand; it really doesn't occur to me. I'm just focused on my horse, my job, my course.

—Leslie Howard, Olympic show jumping gold and silver
medalist, World Cup Finals champion

Ride Exercises with Bookends

Have you heard the old Pop Warner quote "You play the way you practice"? This is particularly apropos to how you train your focus.

Why would anyone think that they could be unfocused and chatting with friends in lessons, restart or redo an exercise numerous times in training, rely on their trainer for constant instruction during a test or course—and then be focused and stellar when they so chose? For instance, at a horse show? As a rider, you must look for opportunities to practice intensifying your focus as you train from day to day.

Just focus on one or two things rather than trying to do everything perfectly. I always tell [students] it's not practice that makes perfect and it's not really perfect practice that makes perfect. It's the attempt at perfect practice that keeps you focused and on your way to success. Keep trying. Perfection is elusive but you will find satisfaction in the journey.

—Melanie Smith Taylor, Olympic show jumping
gold medalist

As an example, let's say the dressage instructor you clinic with regularly wants you to improve the accuracy of your tests by concentrating on "leg first" for all downward transitions, and you have a dressage show in two weeks. Your homework is simple: Prepare early, leg to hand; be accurate and sharp. You decide to design an exercise with a four-loop serpentine, with trot/walk transitions across the centerline on your first way across the ring, and canter/walk transitions on the way back. You have integrated your trainer's homework and created a very simple schooling exercise.

The idea here is for you to go one step further and give yourself very precise "bookends" for riding the drill: a clear beginning and a clear ending. Why? Here are the benefits:

- An intensified focus

- A reminder to stay in the moment and ride through any challenges that crop up

- An opportunity to practice your pre-ride routine (what you do and say to yourself right before you begin)

- A clear transition from your assessment/analysis of what needs to happen to the performance phase of the ride (that requires an enhanced mind-body connection)

- A designated time to concentrate on problem solving and reviewing the ride once you have finished the exercise

Riding exercises with bookends can be done with flatwork, all or part of a dressage test, cavaletti, or jumping work. Whether your "courses" are simple or complex, the key is the way you frame the exercise and the attention you pay to your focus throughout.

Here is how to ride an exercise with bookends:

1. **Set up.** Choose a clear beginning and ending point for the exercise or course by selecting or creating a marker of some sort—two cones, or two standards, a specific fence post, a particular jump, or the in-gate to the ring. Occasionally, especially before a show, actually entering the ring and exiting on conclusion of the exercise is useful as well. By entering and exiting, you mimic the competition environment and practice your pre-ride process more fully.

2. **Begin.** After you have warmed up and feel ready to begin, come to a halt at your marker(s). Look in at the ring and make a clearly defined plan for riding your exercise. Your focus should be at a level similar to your intensity at a show or event. Think about adding your "homework" into your course plan; you are adding *how* you will ride well to *what* you will ride (from our earlier example, you would be thinking, "Leg to hand, accurate and sharp."). Take two deep, complete breaths—in through your nose, out through your mouth—and transition from the "planning/analysis" phase of your ride to the riding portion.

3. **Ride your exercise.** Begin the exercise and stay completely in the present moment. You are riding your plan and incorporating what you feel from your horse. Be sure to use training solutions as you ride through the whole exercise; don't allow yourself to reflect back or critique your progress during this phase.

4. **Finish and review.** When you get to your markers at the end of your exercise, halt, and then be disciplined about thinking first of at least two things you liked, such as your first canter transition, how your eye stayed up and ahead of you, or the accuracy of your trot transitions on the centerline. Next, review the ride

from beginning to end and look for places to improve, trying not to allow any negative emotions or self-talk to creep into your thinking. Reviewing and evaluating only at the conclusion of each section will build the mental strength and discipline to stay in the moment.

Riding with bookends is a strategy you can do on your own when schooling or hacking your horse, or as a purely mental tool within a lesson (obviously scaling back the use of start and finish markers to fit seamlessly into your trainer's lesson plan). The more opportunities you give yourself to practice with a heightened focus, the stronger and more skilled your focus will be when it truly counts.

A TOP TIP

Train your focus the way you train your horse:
Follow a routine, use simple instructions, and
be aware of every moment.

Chapter Highlights
Tools to Enhance Focus

✔ Focus on things within your control.

✔ Use cue words and checkpoints to direct your focus to the present moment.

✔ Create thorough ride plans.

✔ Ride exercises with bookends to build control over your focus.

4

Vision

Developing Skills Through
Visualization and Observation

MASTERING ANY SKILL requires vision. A vision of what you want to create, an idea of what you want the end result to be. With respect to being the best rider you can become, what is your vision? In partnership with your horse, do you seek to display elegance, partnership, joy, excitement, brilliance, precision, expertise, or _____? Having a clear vision is essential for your mind and body to remain on the same page, constantly striving for the same goals.

In riding, you can find many opportunities to develop your vision through observation, as well as to use your mind's eye to imagine and visualize what you want to happen in your own rides. Increasing your skill, improving the harmony you have with your horse, and achieving greater consistency are all benefits of enhancing your vision.

Building Your Vision

Hopefully you have a clear vision of what you would like to create as a rider. Before you dive into the strategies presented here, it would be a good idea to assess your starting point. How much do you already use visualization and observation? Measure your use of these tools by thinking through the following questions:

- Do you visualize regularly? Why or why not?

- What do you imagine when you visualize?

- When do you do it?

- Why do you believe visualizing is useful?

- When and where do you watch other riders?

- Why do you think observing others is useful to your own riding?

- How do you use the information you get from watching skilled riders?

Most of the riders I work with report that they actively watch a lot of riders as well as visualize, which is terrific. If this is you, give yourself full credit for making a positive effort to prepare effectively and learn as much as possible. You're building a vision of what you want to create when you ride, thus getting you ever closer to your ultimate goals.

To be sure, visualization is the most talked-about and utilized sport psychology skill. However, in my travels working with clients, I hear a lot of thinly veiled negative comments such as, "I do it, but the ride itself never goes *exactly* like I visualize it." Wait a second, how could it? You aren't a machine, and neither is your horse. That's like riding beautifully in a lesson and then saying, "What if I don't ride *exactly* like that at the show next week?" That question misses the main point, which is that the beautiful ride in the lesson *significantly increased* the likelihood of riding well. Period. Visualization is likewise a practice tool and happens to be the most powerful mental training technique for improving your focus, reaction time, physical skill, and mind-body connection (sorry to say, it doesn't come with a guarantee to predict the future like a crystal ball!).

Misconceptions and worry about visualization and observation are plentiful. Here are several other examples:

- "I keep making mistakes when I visualize!"
- "When I watch great riders, it always looks so different from what I do. It gets a little depressing."
- "I get so distracted when I try to visualize."
- "I always heard you were supposed to visualize right before you go to sleep—but it makes me fall asleep!"
- "I never have time to visualize."
- "When I watch someone make a mistake, I get scared I'm going to go out and do the same thing."

The goals for this chapter are to bust through some misconceptions about visualization and observation, teach you the basics of how to visualize, fine-tune your skills, and show you how to observe others productively. At the end, you will be able to use visualization and observation to build muscle memory and mental strength, and to inspire you to greater heights.

Visualization

There goes Natalie, finishing her warm-up and heading to the arena, about to ride her first dressage test at a show. Natalie is a new adult rider who practiced and practiced the movements, but has only ridden through the entire test three times so her mare would not anticipate the movements. Her family is there to cheer her on, she knows her husband is going to video her, and she really wants to ride a great test. Although she has every right to be incredibly nervous, her confidence and poise are remarkable. How did she do it?

Turns out, she has been visualizing the test in its entirety for weeks. She even went to the facility where the show is being held so she could imagine herself in the very environment she's in right now. Natalie has watched tons of lessons with people who ride at higher levels, and has seen video of people riding the test she is about to perform. She feels like her mental practice has given her the boost she needs to ride her very best when it counts. Well done, Natalie! But wait, *how did she do it?*

VISUALIZATION: HOW IT WORKS

The human body cannot tell the difference between a real event and a vividly imagined one. Therefore, each time you visualize a ride (using all your senses so you actually feel as if you're in the saddle), your body is learning how to execute the mental and physical requirements of that test, course, or exercise. How does it work? Visualization creates a template for the sequence of mind-body reflexes and reactions contained in the ride, and thus prepares you for what you are going to do.

Visualization builds on what is called "muscle memory." When you have strong muscle memory for a skill (such as asking your horse to pick up the left lead canter or posting on the correct diagonal), it's almost as if your body knows what to do without your having to give it direct, specific instructions. Often this muscle memory comes from a great deal of physical practice and repetition. However, muscle memory is also being built when you visualize. As you visualize, your muscles receive electrical impulses that sync up with the physical event you're creating in your mind. You are therefore teaching your body (and muscles) how to carry out the job your mind is imagining.

By creating vivid images of an upcoming movement/course/exercise/test, you are giving yourself a fantastic opportunity to create an optimal performance. Your mind and body are getting trained (remember that your mind is like a muscle too) to respond accurately to the demands of the ride. Need to gallop and jump in and out of the woods (and deep shade) on your cross-country course? Are you striving to correct your habit of looking down when you jump? Want to improve your horse's impulsion throughout your dressage test? Your mental and physical responses to these situations will be exponentially improved by visualizing in addition to spending time in the saddle.

Visualization: The Basics

Included here are the most important fundamentals to master when learning how to visualize. Remember that it's a skill unto itself—the better you visualize, the better the results. Understanding the following basics ensures your imagery will generate all the benefits this technique has to offer.

- **Vivid images.** Use all of your senses when visualizing because this will allow your body to respond to the situation as it will in real life. The more real the image, the more your body is able to learn. In order to build vividness, think about these questions as you create your imagery:

Visualization is key to meeting your goals.

- ❏ *What do I see?* Such as colors, sizes, and types of jumps, items inside and outside the ring, cross-country terrain, and conditions of the warm-up area.

- ❏ *What do I feel?* Relate this question to every part of your body—legs, hands, seat—as well as your emotions.

- ❏ *What do I hear?* Such as my horse's feet on the grass and the buzz of the event.

Note that smelling and tasting are generally less valuable for riding, but can have particular associations that are helpful.

I see every corner; I see every color of every jump out of each turn, where it is set. And I am looking for my track more than anything else. It's like I am riding it. I feel like I have ridden that course ten times before I have ever actually ridden it. I keep riding it in my mind until I have ridden it perfectly.
   —Susan Hutchison, U.S. show jumping team member

- **Control.** Your images must be in your direct control. You decide the what, when, where, and how of everything that transpires in your visualization. Your horse responds accurately to your aids, you take the track you want, your pace and rhythm feel correct—all the details of your visualization feel right and everything responds seamlessly to your will. You are the star of your visualization and you successfully direct everything from beginning to end.

At the Olympics or a really big, big competition, I get there and look at the external show ring and I really visualize not just any ring, I visualize that ring. Where I go in, where the entrance is, where the judges sit. I ride in my mind through the test. That's

Susan Hutchison on Cantano.

how I visualize. I go through the whole ride and I do that several times in the days coming up. But then on the day [I show] I don't. Once I'm preparing on the day I'm done with that, and I concentrate on what I have underneath me.

—Guenter Seidel, three-time Olympic
dressage bronze medalist

- **Internal perspective.** It is best to look through your own eyes when you visualize. See the tips of your horse's ears, the ring or terrain ahead of you, and what you are approaching just as if you were sitting in the saddle. This perspective optimizes the mind-body connection and is the best way to build muscle memory.

  Remember that your body cannot tell the difference between

a real and vividly imagined event. So, for example, when you imagine increasing the contact and adding your leg for your horse to go from a canter to a walk at "C," your body triggers those specific muscle groups that will carry out that action in real life. You have just performed a high-quality "rep" of a beautiful downward transition, making it all the more likely that it will happen smoothly the next time you ask for one on your horse.

What does it feel like as you're riding up to that jump? It's like I'm sitting on the horse looking at the jump, approaching the ditch. Or I feel it with dressage movements. I'm coming into this corner, what does it feel like to sit up and do a half-halt . . . actually feel what my body is going to be doing? You're getting the physical sensation because obviously muscle memory is such a huge part of it. You can visualize what that muscle memory feels like. If you ride through the test you think about how you're setting up for that turn or how you're setting up for the half-pass, how you're positioning the horse's body.

—Gina Miles, Olympic three-day eventing silver medalist

Visualization Basics

- Make your visualization as vivid as possible—feel, sight, sound, emotion, environment—just like the real thing.

- Control your images so they do what you want them to do.

- Look through your own eyes in your imagery.

- Make your visualization move at the same speed as real life.

- Focus on success in your visualization.

- **Real time.** Your visualization happens at the same speed as it would in real life. Your pace, the dimensions of the riding area, and the demands of the exercise are all examples of things that will play a part in determining the time it takes to do the visualization. There is copious research in sports such as swimming, skiing, and running that shows elite athletes are able to visualize each moment of a race down to the second. Why is this important?

Imagine we are ringside at your next event, about to visualize your Training Level stadium round. You prepared appropriately for your imagery session: You were in a quiet location, you had taken some deep breaths, and I said, "Begin." Thirty-four seconds later you said, "I'm done."

Thirty-four seconds? Really? Did you calmly walk through the in-gate? Did you focus through each turn, riding your course plan? Did you finish and walk out of the arena with a positive emotional response, giving your horse a big pat on the neck? I think we would both agree, probably not. For your body to get the most out of visualization, you must create a truly lifelike experience.

Know it, ride it in your mind's eye a few times. And if the time allowed is seventy-eight seconds, it should take you seventy-eight seconds to go over it.

—Missy Clark, top hunter/jumper/equitation trainer

Before a test, I always take a moment and imagine riding the whole test, really feeling the riding and reacting to what I think that particular horse will do. If I can, I'll sit on a tack trunk and close my eyes to visualize before; if I have back-to-back rides, you'll often see me doing my walk warm-up with a glazed expression.

My husband, unbeknownst to me, videotaped me sitting on a tack trunk visualizing at the Olympics. I had my eyes closed nearly the time it takes to do a test.

—Courtney King-Dye, Olympic dressage rider/trainer

Developing Your Visualization Skills

Help! What Do I Do If My Images Won't Do What I Say?

- *Use video of yourself* to jump-start the visualization process. Watch the video and then visualize what you have just seen by switching to an internal perspective and seeing it as if you are re-riding it in your mind. For this process, it is best to use sections of video that contain successful performances.

- *Visualize small sections* of your test or course as you gain control of your images. Better to do short sections well than the whole ride at low quality.

- *Re-create successful moments* in a lesson, show, or schooling session by visualizing them soon after you finish your ride. Be sure to include the positive emotions associated with the experience.

- *While on your horse at the halt,* visualize something you just rode well, or create a visualization for something you are about to do. When you're actually riding, you will be able to practice joining the genuine physical sensations with a vivid mental image.

- **Successful rides.** Be sure to create successful rides in your visualizations. You ride the movements smoothly, jumping the jumps clean, and your horse participates as you wish. As you visualize, let yourself enjoy what it feels like to ride well and achieve your goals. View any errors (whether they are habitual or surprisingly unexpected) as welcome opportunities to reprogram your response to the situation. Simply go back and successfully ride that section again. Therefore, instead of pretending that the mistake didn't occur, you proactively ride the solution and feel a successful outcome (see the next section for more on visualizing solutions).

Fine-Tune Your Visualization Skills

Do the visualization basics sound familiar to you? Are you routinely visualizing after lessons, rides, and shows to cement your successes as well as visualizing ahead of time to prepare for upcoming rides? If so, terrific! However, just like a Formula 1 racecar, even people who are performing well can benefit from a tune-up now and again. What follows are a variety of subtle tweaks and suggestions that pack a lot of power.

1. **Create a suitable environment.** Being the busy and well-rounded person you are, you probably need to visualize at a variety of times and places. Do your best to be somewhere you won't be disturbed, and take some relaxing and focusing breaths when you begin. Being left alone may require some ingenuity on your part, such as camping out in your car at a show or wearing headphones so you won't be disturbed.

2. **Sit in position.** Practice your imagery in a position similar to the one you have when riding. This will help to ensure that

visualization is an active process for you (not passive, like sitting back and watching a movie). Sit with correct and tall posture at the front of your chair, put both feet flat on the ground hip width apart, and hold your hands lightly in your lap as if they were holding reins. This will help the appropriate muscle groups activate when they need to, keep you fresh and focused, and help you feel like you're in the driver's seat of your imagery.

When I go over the course with [students], I really [want them to] feel the jump . . . What does it feel like to jump the five-foot vertical? What does it feel like to jump the triple bar? Really giving it the feeling and the sensitivity and all that stuff as you do the visualization . . . How are the seven [strides] to the water jump? You've got to stay out, wait, and then you go. As you're [visualizing] . . . you feel it.

—Anne Kursinski, five-time Olympic show jumper,
two-time Olympic silver medalist

3. **Use equipment.** There are many ways to integrate physical props into your mental rehearsal to enhance the richness of your visualization experience. Sitting on an exercise ball, holding onto reins, and/or wearing some riding clothes (shirt with collar, tall boots) are all examples of things that can round out your imagination. They will help kick-start your muscle memory to make your images more vivid and lifelike, tremendously strengthening the usefulness of the exercise.

4. **Include positive emotion.** Attach strong positive feelings to your imagery, particularly as you imagine finishing your ride. This will build muscle memory that includes expectations of emotions such as excitement and happiness. For example, imagine yourself

giving your horse a big pat on the neck as you canter across the finish line, a smile on your face, feeling the exhilaration of a job well done. These positive, emotional expectations can greatly affect your attitude and decision-making during your ride.

5. **Integrate performance goals.** Let's say one of your major goals for your next event is to look early and keep your reins short in your stadium round. Your visualization can help you take control and focus on these performance goals (see chapter 2) by imagining yourself accomplishing them at particular checkpoints within your course plan (see chapter 3). Decide where your checkpoints will occur on course before you begin your visualization, then feel yourself closing your fingers on the reins to keep them short, with your hands up your horse's neck where they need to be. By adding this specific feel and focus into your imagery sessions, you can fine-tune the training your mind and body receive.

6. **Imagine solutions.** Ride the solution to your and your horse's typical mistakes. You can rest assured that any "bad" habits the two of you have will crop up in many of your visualizations. See this as opportunity! It will give you more chances to practice preventing the mistake and effectively responding to it. Does your horse have a right drift? Visualize yourself anticipating and correcting the problem. Do you tip your upper body forward at the base of wide oxers? Imagine stretching tall as you leave the ground. Think of what action you need to take—with your position, track, pace—to get the job done well and resolve the issue. Take control of the imagery, push the "replay" button, and ride the element again with a positive result. Do not give up until you get it right.

Watch Riders You Admire

How long has it been since you watched riders you truly admired? Where were you? What were they doing on their horse that stood out to you? How did it make you feel to see their talent and quality focus? Hopefully you walked away from the experience feeling inspired and motivated. Equestrian sport provides many opportunities to observe other riders train and compete; it's helpful to identify all the specific ways watching can be a productive endeavor. For example, the next time you're at a horse show, you will probably watch a great deal more than you actually ride—wouldn't it be great to make sure the time is well spent?

Watching riders you admire, in person or on video, deepens your awareness of the physical skills and mental attitudes you want to develop. You may be lucky enough to be surrounded by people you think highly of—maybe you ride at a large barn with a wide range

Watch other riders for inspiration and instruction, and to determine which skills you'd like to develop.

of talent or go to horse shows or events with plenty of divisions and variety. These can be ideal places to find people who are exciting to watch because they have talents and abilities you respect.

When you're watching productively, your goal is to look for people with the specific traits and skills you are striving to attain. You may luck out and find people who have the whole package, or you may want to simply focus on a particular part of a rider—like his or her lower leg position, patience, or ability to remain calm under pressure.

When it's challenging to find occasions to observe riders you admire, remember that technology is a fantastic resource. There have never been so many ways to see video of phenomenal riders from all over the world. You can watch these rides on YouTube and other specialized equestrian websites (some free, some pay-per-view), think them through, and replay to your heart's content!

At times when you watch talented riders, you may find it tough to avoid letting comparison, criticism, and competitiveness get in your way: "She always _____; I don't understand _____; why do the judges _____? I never _____." Any of those sound familiar? Uh-oh! Be very, very careful to not let these types of thoughts waste your energy and brainpower. It's a mental trap to feel threatened by someone who rides with polish and skill (and perhaps to a higher level than you do); instead, make it a priority to adopt an attitude of learning and appreciation when you're observing others. The potential benefits are tremendous, and the philosophy will serve you for your entire riding career.

Another way to watch productively is to pretend you are the person you're observing. Yes, it sounds a little bit funny, but it can be a terrific way to get more quality repetition and practice. In fact, you have probably observed trainers "ride along" with their students as they stood watching. They may have leaned forward as the rider left the ground at a jump, or stretched up and lifted their hand ever so slightly when their student needed to half-halt. This is something that may happen as an accidental result of a trainer watching with passion and empathy, but this scenario is something you can use to your benefit.

The key is to watch with your whole body and sympathize with the rider's situation to the extent that you react to what you are seeing *in the moment.*

Use your creativity and imagination during this process; it will be aided by sitting in a neutral position to observe. A neutral position for this strategy includes planting both feet flat on the ground, sitting evenly on both seat bones, and maintaining your posture without leaning back on your chair. Your muscles will be more receptive and available to react to what you are watching, thus giving you high-quality simulated practice. Often it is helpful to watch and "ride along" with riders who exceed your level of proficiency so you can trust they are modeling exceptional reactions and skills.

You may occasionally watch someone very talented who makes a mistake, or something unexpected happens. Watch carefully to see how the rider handles the situation and gets himself and his horse back on track. Remember excellence is not about perfection, or a 100 percent mistake-free ride. Riders at the top level are simply reacting and adapting to what is happening with lightning speed. Conversely, you may watch riders who don't exemplify the complete picture you are striving for. In those instances, if you can, pick out one or two things that stand out to you as first rate.

Watching productively will have the added benefit of building your visualization skills. You will be practicing allowing an image to trigger physical responses in your body. This is good! It is deepening your mind-body connection and your ability to use this synthesis at will. Remember that visualization is a skill like any other—the more ways you have to develop it the better.

I encourage my kids to watch any of the top riders on the com-
puter list in the schooling area. To actually watch their facial
focus when they're schooling and especially when they go in the
ring. Or, I tell them to watch top tennis players, top golfers, top
athletes—to watch their focus. If you watch McLain or Beezie,
you can just see the body language; you can see the facial focus.
If you can put yourself in that position, you have to be ahead of
the game.

—Leslie Howard, Olympic show jumping gold and silver
medalist, World Cup Finals champion

The Outside-In Principle

Now let's imagine you have spent some time watching productively
at your barn, at your last horse show, and even online when you have
had some spare time throughout the day. You've seen a lot of riding
to be sure, some terrific, some average, and some not so great—but
you have made it a point to focus on riders who have at least one
or two skills that are straight-up fantastic.

As a result, it was not a surprise yesterday when you said under
your breath, "I wish I had Sue's poise; she always looks so elegant and
soft. Her strength looks effortless yet rock solid at the same time."
This is the moment you want to capture like a firefly in a jar. In
the brief period you reflect on what you appreciate about her style,
your whole body is listening attentively. Use the moment to paint
a vivid picture in your mind of Sue's position and imagine what it
would feel like to ride like her. By using your mind's eye to create
that vision, you're enabling your body to figure out how to possess
the same skills. Complete the strategy by putting your body in the
same position (your "Outside") to generate the same skills or psychological mind-set (the "Inside").

The Outside-In Principle can help you ride with heightened technical skills as well as build the emotional strength you need to achieve your goals—depending on what you choose to concentrate on when you use it.

GAIN TECHNICAL SKILL

For both inspiration and instruction, find riders to watch who exemplify the physical skills you are striving to attain. For example, you may be trying to build a habit of keeping your hands more in front of your body; your trainer is constantly telling you, "Raise your hands!"

You can watch an elite rider who has beautifully placed, still hands to help you memorize the position, and then file that memory like saving a picture to your laptop. Flash an image of those hands in your mind the next time you go riding and let it guide yours into position.

BUILD PSYCHOLOGICAL POISE

When you see someone's posture, facial expression, and behavior, you unconsciously imagine their thoughts and feelings (confidence, focus, calm, energy, and positivity). Therefore, when you act like them and hold your body in a similar position, by viewing that rider in your mind's eye and then adopting those same positions, you trigger the psychological response you associate with them in that moment.

Ideally, when you're using the Outside-In Principle, you will choose a rider to emulate who has both the physical skill(s) and psychological strength you are striving for so you can get the most "bang for your buck." To demonstrate how powerful this can be, do the following exercise:

1. Think about a specific performance goal related to your

position or use of aids that you are having a tough time accomplishing. You may even have some doubts that it will become a new habit, but it is very important to your progress as a rider.

2. Now choose a rider you admire who possesses that skill day in and day out, and flash the image of them in front of your mind's eye.

3. Next, imagine you are that rider utilizing that skill. Adopt the position that is required and/or activate the parts of your body that are involved. At the same time, lift the top of your head toward the ceiling, open your chest, and pick up your chin. How does it feel to be them?

4. Consider the goal again—what do you notice? Do you feel better prepared to go after it?

Of course there is so much in sport we do not control, but you can control your self-confidence and vision. Smart athletes utilize any strategy they can to build themselves up and go after their goals from a place of strength. Spending time making use of the Outside-In Principle is an example of a strategy that will add to your capabilities.

WHEN TO USE THE OUTSIDE-IN PRINCIPLE

When? Anytime you think of it! (Well, safely and within reason, of course.) Think of this principle as a short-form visualization, a quick way of visiting positive muscle memory that will build your riding talents. Whether or not you're on your horse, you can think of riders to emulate that will develop good habits around your posture, position, and attitude.

So, sitting in commute traffic? Standing in line to get your coffee?

Waiting for your turn to school the down-bank during a cross-country school? Walking a circle at the back gate at a horse show? Use the Outside-In Principle to instantaneously trigger those qualities or skills you want to have and ride with. The vision of the person you admire will become a polished touchstone for that physical style and mental strength.

A TOP TIP

Your imagination creates momentum like an electrical storm. The instant you have a vision in mind, your body is already on its way to making it come true.

Chapter Highlights
Visualizing Effectively

✔ Learn the basic keys for creating effective visualizations, including control and vividness.

✔ Fine-tune your visualizations skills by paying attention to details like your environment,
integrating performance goals, and imagining
solutions.

✔ Watch riders you admire to inspire you and
learn from their experiences.

✔ Use the Outside-In Principle to facilitate physical and psychological poise.

5

Energy

Assess and Adjust Your Energy Level
Then Channel It Wisely

THERE YOU ARE on your horse, waiting for your lesson to start. Things have been very challenging recently, and to say you've been having a rough time is an understatement.

These difficulties are constantly on your mind; in fact, at this point they have created enough anxiety to fill a large wheelbarrow. Today you're feeling particularly off-kilter. You perform a quick self-assessment and this is the worrisome report: "Heart in my throat and can't seem to catch my breath. Legs are weak like spaghetti. Arms are tight and strangely lifeless. I'm imagining nothing but mistakes!"

You pause and then think the truly scary thought, "I love riding my horse, but right now I am wondering why I am even here." Uh-oh! Houston, we have a problem. Riding is supposed to be fun. What happened?

There can be times when your mental and physical energy feels out of control, as if you're a small boat being tossed around on a sea of adrenalin. Extra energy in your body can take strength away from places that need it, and add too much of a charge to areas that need to be supple and relaxed. Understandably, this can be quite frustrating, but changing your perspective about what energy is and what it can do for you is the golden ticket to finding your way to shore.

To start adjusting and successfully utilizing mental and physical energy, you must do just that: Simply call it energy. You may have too much or you may have too little—either way you do yourself a disservice by vilifying the state you're experiencing. It is just a state of being, and with practice and the proper techniques, you can learn to effectively control it. Then, instead of getting stuck judging how you feel with a negative label like "nervous," "anxious," "tired," "flat," "zoned-out"—as if that is a state you are trapped in and have no control over—you can spend your time getting yourself to the energy level you need. This will happen in one of two ways:

1. **Let go of the energy you don't need, then channel the rest productively.** You can learn to release unneeded energy and effectively direct the rest to help you accomplish your goals. Remember this at the moment your energy is spiking; your body is on your team, trying to help. Sure, it may be a bit overzealous, but energy in its pure state represents your body's readiness to get the job done. It's a bit like the engineer's assistant in an old steam train throwing too much coal on the fire. Ideally, the head engineer simply says, "Thanks for your help, but this is a bit more than we need. I am going to let off some steam here at the station, and we'll use the rest to get us to Chicago."

2. **Generate energy for the focus and intensity you need to ride your best.** When you are tired, unfocused, underwhelmed, or

generally feeling blah, you may need to boost your energy level to ride your best, and there are many strategies that can help you.

First, assess your current state and be clear about the energy level you're going for—which is your Optimal Energy Zone—and then choose the most appropriate tools to utilize in that moment. Ideally (and with practice), it will feel like your energy is on tap, and anytime you need to, you can either make more or draw on your reserves.

Remind yourself that you do in fact (1) need your energy and (2) have control over it. These are important steps in becoming a consistent rider. You simply assess your energy level, choose the best tools to adjust it appropriately, and away you go.

I definitely, still to this day, can get nervous or worked up. You don't always realize that nervous is good [but] really it is at those shows when it's back east or major shows or major competitions that I always seem to ride better. So the nervousness and then knowing how to work it . . . that's when you ride your best.
—John French, three-time World Champion Hunter Rider,
U.S. show jumping team member

Your Optimal Energy Zone

Personality, experience, fitness, level, and what discipline(s) you participate in are just a few of the variables that will affect how much is the "right" amount of energy to have in a particular riding situation. The purpose of this chapter is to help you understand and learn to manage *your* mental and physical energy so you can ride your best. Therefore, this won't be a lesson to teach you all the different kinds of engines and how they work, but just your unique make and model.

So let's get cracking on the assessment tool, definition, and discussion of your Optimal Energy Zone.

PERFORMANCE-ENERGY ASSESSMENT SCALE

No one can tell you the exact amount of energy you need or what it feels like—this is information you have to gather yourself. Use the Performance-Energy Assessment Scale on page 85 to rate where you typically find yourself in your day-to-day riding.

This scale is based on the Inverted-U Hypothesis and Individualized Zone of Optimal Functioning, which are sport psychology models of arousal and performance. The Inverted-U Hypothesis predicts that as arousal (or energy, for our purposes here) increases from low to high, the rider's performance progressively increases. An optimal level of energy and best possible performance are achieved at a certain point, which varies by individual. If energy continues to increase past that optimal point, performance will decrease, either slowly or dramatically, again depending on the individual.

Here is what the numbers mean:

- The numbers 1–4 depict energy that is below optimal: You feel varying degrees of tired, flat, lethargic, weak, and unfocused. This results in a subpar performance.

- The number 5 depicts your ideal level of energy that creates your best performance: You are feeling strong, energized, and focused. It's your Optimal Energy Zone.

- The numbers 6–9 depict energy that is too high: You feel nervous, tight, and stressed, creating a performance that is less than your best.

Notice the differences in your energy between your hacks, lessons, and shows:

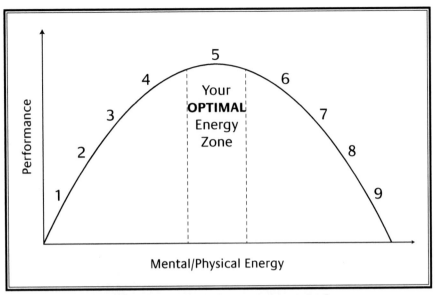

Performance-Energy Assessment Scale

1. Put an "H" on the graph where your energy typically is when you ride/hack on your own.

2. Put an "L" where your energy is during a lesson.

3. Put an "S" where your energy tends to be when you're riding at a show.

As you rate your energy levels, ask yourself these questions:

- **What happens to my riding skills when I have too little energy?** How can you tell you "don't have it"? What changes in your technical riding abilities, muscles, awareness, and mental attitude?

- **What does it feel like to have too much energy when I'm riding?** What different feelings do you recognize when you are too

The Goldilocks Guide to Understanding Your Energy

As you read through the common causes and performance symptoms associated with different energy levels, be sure to add your own ideas or experiences in the blank spaces. Remember, there are no universal "right" answers; this is a guide to help you understand your own process and then use the knowledge to gain more control over your energy.

Too Much Energy (6–9*)

Potential Causes:

1. Fear response to a challenging situation
2. Performance anxiety
3. Self-doubt
4. _____

Typical Symptoms:

1. Shallow, irregular, or rapid breathing
2. Holding your breath
3. Increased muscle tension
4. Tunnel vision
5. Impairment of reflexes
6. Feeling physically weak
7. Negative self-talk
8. _____

amped up? You may interpret this experience as nervousness, anxiety, or worry, but what does it do to your body, focus, and thoughts? What changes do you notice most?

- **What does my energy feel like when I am at a 5 and in my Optimal Energy Zone?** This is key! You need to understand what it feels like to be in your zone so you will know what you're shooting for, and how to identify it when you are there. Without

Too Little Energy (1–4*)

Potential Causes:

1. Fatigue
2. Boredom
3. Distraction
4. _____

Typical Symptoms:

1. Physical weakness
2. Lack of or diffused focus
3. Poor planning
4. Slow reactions
5. _____

Just Right Energy (5*)

Potential Causes:

1. Excellent preparation
2. Confidence in abilities
3. Clear goals
4. Positive attitude and inter- actions with others
5. Enjoyment
6. _____

Typical Symptoms:

1. Focused in the moment
2. Appropriate vision for task
3. Flexible
4. Regular, deep breathing
5. Tall, balanced posture
6. _____

*Note: These numbers refer to the range of energy you feel as presented on the Performance-Energy Assessment Scale.

this knowledge, you can adjust your energy all you want and still miss the mark, like an archer shooting arrows in the dark. What do you feel physically when you're at a 5? What are your thoughts about? How do you feel emotionally?

ENERGY LEVELS AND FEELINGS

Now take a look at "The Goldilocks Guide to Understanding Your Energy" above. It describes the typical indicators of having too much, too little, or just the right amount of energy to further assist you in your identification process. Goldilocks discovered what "just right!" felt like, and you can too. Here, you will learn not only what optimal energy is but also how to make it for yourself.

Before you build a personalized preparation routine, it's not unusual to have differences in your energy level when you are either riding on your own, in lessons, or at shows. For example, you may be at a 3–4 energy level in hacks and lessons, and in the 6–7 range at shows. This is very common, but doesn't do much to prepare you to handle your extra energy or ride well at your competitions. However, never forget that knowledge is power. Once you know what your typical energy pattern is, you can put things in place within your preparation routine that will help you ride at a 5 as much as possible. For you to have true consistency in your riding, you must also have consistency in your energy. The rest of the chapter will explore tools you can use to adjust it.

> *I just had a girl do her first grand prix indoors, probably her fourth grand prix ever. She said, "I'm really nervous!" And I said, "That's good. You should be nervous; anyone who is at the in-gate who tells you they aren't nervous is full of it. It's just a matter of maintaining the adrenalin level to make it work for you, and not against you."*
> —Susan Hutchison, U.S. show jumping team member

Breathing: Your Best Energy Adjuster

On a bright spring day, I went to an event to observe Ava, a client who had come to me because she was battling her nerves before and during her stadium rounds. She reported that she frequently held her breath on course and half joked that one day she might actually pass out. The show environment got Ava's energy up to extremely high levels, and she was struggling to cope. We had just started working together, and although I knew some basic things about her (she was in her late twenties, fit, motivated, new to eventing, and eager to move up to Novice Level in the fall), I hadn't seen her ride.

As I observed Ava, I noticed that while she was at the back gate waiting to go, she spoke so softly to her trainer she was barely audible. Her eyebrows were up by her helmet, and her shoulders were up toward her ears. Tension and worry were reflected in her round face from top to bottom. Her ride clearly reflected this tension (let's just say that there was more than one gasp from her support team as she cantered around the course).

She came out of the ring struggling to catch her breath, looked at me, and said, "Help!" I nodded. It was obvious to me that before, during, and after Ava's round, her breathing had been very irregular; this would be our starting point (see Ava's complete energy-management plan at the end of this chapter).

Breathing is one of the easiest ways to control the body's physical

Concentrated practice will help you learn breathing techniques.

and physiological state, partially because with the proper mindfulness and technique, it is simply easy to do. When you breathe deeply, you help oxygenate your blood and remove any accumulated toxins in your cells that are getting in your way. This helps your body relax, settle, and, if necessary, come out of flight-or-fight mode that can be caused by fear or stress (when you are in fight-or-flight mode, adrenaline has kicked in to the point where there is too much energy, and it is at risk of inhibiting your performance). Additionally, your mind associates confidence with smooth, rhythmic breathing.

Although breathing is essential for optimal performance, it is an unconscious process. Therefore, it is frequently taken for granted or overlooked when it comes to preparation or the skills associated with peak performance. When you're riding, your breathing may change unintentionally in many ways:

- Intense concentration can cause you to dramatically alter your breathing. In an attempt to reduce distraction and direct all your energy to the highest-priority task (jumping the technical aspects of a course well, getting through a difficult series of movements in a test, listening intently to your trainer's instructions), you may attempt to maintain your body's status quo, causing things to lock up—including your chest and lungs.

- When you are nervous or scared, your fight-or-flight response gets triggered. This may cause you to curl up and go into some approximation of the fetal position. In this case, your upper body, chest, and lungs are essentially folded, making it very difficult to take a complete, full breath.

- Being out of breath due to lack of cardio fitness can be misinterpreted as an inability to perform the task at hand. In this case, lack of physical fitness creates a change in your breathing, which then breeds doubt, which then snowballs into a lack of confidence that changes how you ride.

- When you're facing a challenge you perceive as stressful, shallow breathing can cause a lack of oxygen and create a negative feedback loop like this:

  1. You're concerned about the riding challenge you're facing.

  2. Your breath gets shallow and fast.

  3. You feel out of breath.

  4. This worries you.

  5. The worry makes you breathe even more shallow and fast.

  6. You get more out of breath—and so it continues.

- When you are bored or "flat," you can easily forget to integrate your breathing into your ride as you normally would, thus exacerbating the problem. It makes sense that when you aren't feeling sharp, you can overlook the things that maintain your energy, focus, and intensity. The old chicken-and-egg scenario!

- Ask yourself, What happens to my breathing when I'm feeling nervous? Fearful? Extremely tired? Weak? In those situations, your breathing may in fact be affected, and not for the better. Has someone ever said to you, "Take a deep breath!" "Keep breathing!" "Relax and breathe!" or "Get focused with a breath." Were those reminders helpful? Well, they were definitely on the right track.

Again, breathing is certainly the best and easiest way to adjust your energy level, but you still need to utilize a method for it to get the results you want. Of all the breathing techniques, a specific breathing strategy called Circle Breathing can really improve your use of your breath.

Circle Breathing

Circle Breathing is a foundational technique used to increase or decrease your energy level, build confidence, and improve focus. The emphasis is on breathing from the diaphragm (or belly) instead of the chest and consciously controlling the sequence of the breath, since these produce feelings of being centered and in control.

Here are the directions for a Circle Breath:

1. **Inhale through your nose while counting to three.** Open your chest and lift your chin. Bring air into your lungs from top to bottom and breathe energy in. Feel your belly expand as if you are inflating a balloon.

2. **Pause while counting to two.** Allow yourself this moment to feel still, calm, and patient.

3. **Exhale gently through your mouth at a steady rate while counting to four.** Be sure that your exhale lasts for at least a beat longer than your inhale. Feel your belly flatten, and the muscles in your face and arms relax, while your body melts gently toward the ground. Let yourself enjoy this peaceful moment.

4. **Appreciate how grounded and strong you feel.** And then begin your next Circle Breath.

REDUCE YOUR ENERGY (RELAXATION)

When relaxation (or letting go of extra energy) is the primary goal for the Circle Breath, pay the most attention to the exhalation through your mouth. Gently purse your lips and imagine any tense muscles in your body letting go as you exhale the used air from your stomach and up each level of your lungs. Pay special attention to smoothly exhaling for a beat or two longer than you inhaled. You may even attach an image to the process, like visualizing butterflies flying out of your mouth (a useful way to feel a sense of control and empowerment over your nervousness/extra energy). In addition, think of a word or phrase associated with being calm and centered that you say to yourself as you exhale, such as "Let go," "Easy," "Balance," or "Relax."

INCREASE YOUR ENERGY

When you find yourself needing to increase your energy level, you will concentrate most on your inhale. Fix your gaze on a specific point while you inhale purposefully through your nose—this will narrow and therefore intensify your resolve. To turn up the volume on your energy, imagine breathing in strength. As you inhale, you may choose a vibrant color to bring into your lungs, such as a brilliant blue or shimmering gold.

It's also helpful to pull up a memory of a time you fought through fatigue or dug deep to "get it done"—this could even be from other life experiences or athletic endeavors. This can be an inspiring reminder that not only does your determination play a large role in your success, but you have done it before, and you can do it again. Having a cue word or phrase to associate with increasing your energy can also be valuable, such as "Now," "Power," or "Get it!"

WHEN AND WHERE TO USE CIRCLE BREATHING

Anytime you're learning a new strategy, it is helpful to brainstorm the specifics of where and when you will use it. By doing this ahead of time, you increase the likelihood of working it into your routine. Of course you would like for Circle Breathing to be something you can pull out of your toolbox on the fly as you need it, but you have to practice the process and foster your belief that it will actually work.

You know more about your typical energy levels now after using the Performance-Energy Assessment Scale, so go ahead and make a list of several times and places you could use Circle Breathing this week to increase or decrease your energy before, during, or after your rides. How about . . .

- While standing on the mounting block?

- When waiting your turn at the back gate at a show?

- During a walk break in the ninety-five-degree sunshine of a summer lesson?

Note: Be careful to come up with times you have a moment to concentrate on yourself, because this process requires an internal focus. For example, using Circle Breathing while halted or when walking your horse is fine, but do not do it while trotting, cantering, or jumping.

A Shortened Version

Have you ever held your breath during a ride or come out of the show ring gasping for breath? Have you ever realized your breathing was a bit strange on course or during your test? Although Circle Breathing in its entirety is too much to attend to, you can shorten the process for the ring. Exhaling consciously through your mouth is a way to bring quality breathing into the ride with you.

This method requires less internal thought while still guaranteeing you're continuing to breathe well, because you cannot physically exhale without having inhaled some (hopefully fresh) air. You can remember to do this by creating checkpoints throughout your course, exercise, or test where you use a cue word like "Breathe." (See chapter 3 for more on checkpoints and cue words.)

It's Mental Strength
Not Just "Relaxation"

Olympic show jumping gold medalist Melanie Smith Taylor describes how competing in a triathlon taught her about calling on mental strength, not relaxation, to get through a stressful competitive challenge.

"Since I do so much teaching now, I have come to realize you cannot ask someone to 'relax' with any success. Relaxation is impossible without a certain degree of confidence. I competed in some triathlons for the first time in 2010. I have been a runner for a long time, but not a swimmer, so I had really put in the miles in the pool in preparation.

"A huge storm front passed through on the morning of my first event and there was actually white water and waves on the normally quiet reservoir. I thought, 'You know what, I could actually drown out here.' For the first time in my life, I felt afraid in a competition. I thought, 'OK, I've got to call on all my years of riding experience and stay focused because I am in uncharted territory.' I had to calm my mind, because it was not a matter of whether I could physically swim the distance. I knew I was prepared. It became mind over matter.

"I must admit that was the most difficult thing I have ever done in sports because of the mental control required. I really feared I could easily drown. As I was trying to swim that day, I acknowledged that it was impossible to say to myself, 'Oh, just relax.' I realize that as a teacher, you cannot tell that to someone . . . if you have physical fear, you cannot relax. You have to overcome it another way. You have to stay strong in your mind and block out the physical fear."

Centering

You've had the feeling: You are balanced and aligned with your horse, your movements together feel almost effortless, and your body is technically correct and in position to help your horse maximize

his efforts. These are feelings of being *centered with* your horse. There is also a technique, presented here, that helps you *center within yourself* so you can more efficiently adjust your energy and focus, and then join harmoniously with your horse. This centering puts your focus in the present moment, regulates your breath, and adjusts your energy. Energy can then be channeled from your center with positive purpose and specific direction, helping you use your aids more effectively.

To center, you will focus your attention and create a reservoir of energy in the center of gravity in your body; this center is a point

Melanie Smith Taylor on Calypso.

just below and behind your belly button. With practice, centering will improve your focus and concentration, and help you ride with confidence.

Here are the directions for centering:

1. **Stand with feet shoulder width apart, arms loosely at your sides, knees slightly bent.**

2. **Use three Circle Breaths to begin.** Exhale away all the events

of the day. Feel your awareness align with your body in the present moment. Release and let go of anything you're holding in your jaw, neck, shoulders, and chest.

3. **Begin centering visualization.** Imagine you are standing outside on a bright, sunny day. It is warm and there is a gentle breeze. Visualize the sun high in the sky overhead. Rays of brilliant sunlight are approaching your body, getting smaller and more powerful as they do so. With the accuracy of a laser beam, the sunlight enters your body at your center, just below your belly button. The energy then radiates up and down your body from your center (which is your own "sun.") You now have a reservoir of strength to anchor your body, from which you can draw energy when you need it.

4. **Now use an image to help deepen your feelings of centeredness.** Feel yourself becoming a majestic oak tree with the trunk as your center, the roots growing down through your feet, and branches stretching up tall through your shoulders and head. Lengthen your spine and open your chest; appreciate how balanced, tall, and centered you feel.

5. **Feel your energy level at an optimal level 5.** Your focus is now precisely in the moment, and all your mental and physical skills are on point to join with your horse. You are ready to perform at your peak, prepared to face any riding challenge before you.

With practice, this process can be shortened to the point where one Circle Breath will get you centered. It is incredibly helpful to practice on your feet or sitting down when you have time throughout your normal day, as well as in the saddle anytime you have the opportunity at the halt or walk.

Additional Breathing Techniques for Adjusting Energy*

Rhythmic Breathing

This technique will help you stay in the moment. Use it when you have downtime and need to maintain your energy level.

1. Inhale through your nose while counting to four.

2. Pause, and count to four.

3. Exhale through your mouth while counting to four.

4. Pause and be still, counting to four.

1:2 Ratio Breathing

This powerful technique can help you relax. It's also useful for rest or falling to sleep.

1. Inhale to a count of four.

2. Exhale to a count of eight.

   Note: If you run out of breath before reaching eight, try to take a deeper breath next time and exhale more slowly.

5-to-1 Count

1. Inhale through your nose, pause, say "Five" to yourself, and exhale through your mouth.

2. Inhale through your nose, pause, say "Four" to yourself and "I'm more relaxed at four than I was at five," then exhale through your mouth.

3. Continue counting down in sequence with each breath until you arrive at one.

*Adapted from Williams, *Applied Sport Psychology*, 251–253.

WHEN TO CENTER

Centering will facilitate quality posture, energy, focus, confidence, and breathing. As with many of the strategies presented in this book, it can be adapted to meet a variety of situations and needs. Spend a moment now to think of some times during your last few rides that you could have used a subtle tweak to any of the above factors. For example, perhaps you felt yourself leaning forward, heart beating rapidly, as you watched your trainer raise the jumps in your lesson last Saturday. This reaction changed the location of your center of gravity as it rose up into your chest and affected your balance on your horse. Maybe you wanted a boost of confidence as you walked your horse into the start box at your last event. You may have had concerns from your long workday flying through your head as you tacked up your horse for a nice trail ride yesterday afternoon. Any of those situations would be ideal times to take a couple of breaths to adjust your energy, fix your posture, get centered in the moment, and become prepared for the ride.

Additional Strategies

As with any job, sometimes you need a variety of tools to get it done well. Letting go and channeling some of your extra energy is no exception. There will be days when your normal energy-management routine needs freshening up, or time and circumstances require you to be flexible. Experiment with the following strategies to get comfortable with them; you can then make informed choices when you need to relax and make sure that the energy you have is working for you.

- **Use a variety of breathing techniques.** Trying to fall asleep the night before the clinic you have been looking forward to for months? Walking around the show feeling super excited, but it is still four hours before your class or ride time? There are many breathing methods, in addition to Circle Breathing, that are ideal for relaxation. Some of the best ones are Rhythmic Breathing, 1:2 Ratio Breathing, and 5-to-1 Count. They are described in detail on page 98.

- **Perform a brief body scan.** When your energy spikes, do you know where you get tense? All riders have different physical responses to that phenomenon that can obstruct their skills in the saddle. To scan your body, start at the top of your head and work your way down your body, stopping to release tension in any muscles that feel tight. Release the tension you find by first purposefully tightening those specific muscles (such as your shoulders) for two to four seconds and then slowly releasing and letting go. You'll notice yourself pass by those muscles' starting point of tension as you take them to a greater level of relaxation. You can also do a general body check by shaking out your hands, then rolling your shoulders and neck to get rid of any areas that feel locked up and rigid.

- **Listen to different types of music.** It's a myth to think that over-energized people need to listen to slow, quiet, mellow music (if they listen to any music at all). Be creative! Experiment with listening to a variety of music to see what is most effective for you. Yes, Beethoven's *Moonlight Sonata* or a mellow playlist could be the right call, but you may be surprised to find that cheerful, upbeat music can help you make friends with your energy.

  Listening to something with a good beat and rhythm can make you want to dance, have fun, and go out and perform. Whether it's mellow or upbeat, use music to create positive associations with your energy level; begin to think about enjoying the experience rather than fretting over it. The heart of this idea is that the energy is there, and you're using music to make it an ally.

- **Stretch.** Stretching can help you shape your energy and make it more pliable. Do you partici-pate in any cross-training ac-tivities that you can pull from? Taking your favorite stretches or abbreviated exercises and putting them into your prepa-ration routine, with particu-lar selections for when you're feeling over-energized, can be remarkably effective.

Stretching can help you manage your energy.

Doing some yoga poses in your hotel room before you start your big day at the horse show, stretching out your hamstrings by placing one foot at a time on your tack trunk, and doing arm circles as you walk out to the ring on your horse are all good examples of mindfully moving your body to deepen your aware-ness and be in charge of your energy.

- **Channel your extra energy to your performance goals.** Feeling nervous standing at the back gate before your go? Did you de-cide that your number one performance goal for the show was to keep your lower leg quiet in the air over the jumps? So use that extra energy! Create a short preparatory, sequence of thoughts and movements that will help you focus on achieving that goal.

  For instance, to direct your energy toward accomplishing your goal, take a Circle Breath, step into two-point, anchor more weight in your heel, and secure your lower leg. As you slowly sit back down into the saddle, notice how you now feel confident and secure, instead of nervous and worried, as you walk in the ring and start your opening circle. It is up to you to design a particular sequence to meet your needs; be as creative as the situation allows. This process will help you feel more relaxed because you'll be regaining control over your body's physiological response to the situation and using the energy to enact success strategies for your goals.

I remember saying, "Everybody has nerves, absolutely everybody. Understand that nerves can be used for the positive." I said [to a new, reportedly nervous rider], "How do you know what the difference between nerves and adrenaline is?" I could tell that instantly she was kind of going, "Hmm." I told her that nerves could be turned into positive energy and work for her to get her inspired and motivated.
—Stacia Madden, top hunter/jumper/equitation trainer

Ways to Bring Your Energy Up

Wouldn't it be great if you had a large volume knob for your energy? You could easily read the current level and then turn it up smoothly and efficiently as needed. Here are five great strategies for waking up your mind and body with an added burst of energy:

1. **Focus on what's fun.** Appreciate riding and being with your horse. Shifting your perspective to one of enjoyment can increase your energy by helping you feel a sense of freedom and gratitude for where you are.

2. **Add some physical activity.** It may sound counterintuitive at

first, but this is very effective. With thoughtful, proactive time management, you can shape your riding or competition days to include a small portion of your typical exercise routine.

Taking a short run or a brisk walk around the show grounds before you put on your tall boots, for example, can get your blood moving, activate your mind-body connection, help you take some deep, full breaths, and elevate your energy level.

Having some physical activities you can do anywhere, anytime, is also valuable. For example, the following physical exercise sounds silly (in fact, silliness itself can be an excellent energy booster), but it's surprisingly effective. It goes by many names such as "Silent Applause" or "Penguin Ovation"—you get the idea.

Directions: Stand up straight, with your feet slightly spread. Face the palms of your hands toward each other as if holding a basketball, keep your elbows at your sides. The palms of your hands and your forearms should be relaxed. Begin to move your hands quickly, bringing the palms in turn closer together and then further apart (hence the term "Silent Applause"). The movements should be fast and short, and your hands should never touch. For thirty seconds, make as many movements as possible. Try to have your tempo at about six to eight repetitions per second. This will get you going and wake up your mind and body (don't knock it until you try it!).

3. **Listen to energizing, upbeat music.** Remember hearing your favorite song last week on your way to the barn? What did that do your mood and energy? Listening to something that makes you want to move your body will help you create energy and get you looking for fun in what you're doing. Try to keep music fresh by adding new songs into a playlist and getting ideas from friends, the Internet, or the radio.

4. **Consistently watch your nutrition.** It is difficult (if not practically impossible) to manufacture physical energy out of thin air. If you haven't eaten well for days, your gas tank may be empty, and as talented as you are, you're probably not a magician. To prevent the need for magic, be mindful of what you eat, thereby bringing up your baseline energy over the course of a full day or week.

Eliminate energy sappers like excess sugar, which can cause drastic fluctuations in your blood sugar, resulting in plunging energy levels. Keep enough protein in your diet, especially over the course of a multiday horse show. For example, pack some almonds and raisins for a quick and convenient protein snack. Be careful with coffee and caffeine as they can lead to physical burnout. Drink plenty of water; feelings of dehydration include feeling unfocused, tired, and flat.

You may also want to identify and have on hand your favorite snacks and fluids. Then if you do notice your energy lagging, you can give yourself a quick nutritional boost such as a banana, almond butter sandwich, or electrolyte water.

5. **Paint a mental picture.** What do you feel when you imagine yourself at your next show, championships, medal finals, or a clinic you're looking forward to? Chances are, the very thought of them brings your energy up and perhaps even gets a butterfly or two flying in your stomach. To bring up your "oomph" factor in the moment, you can visualize an important upcoming event, show, or situation. This will allow you to access your passion for riding well and turn it into energy to use now—in the present moment.

For example, if you need to turn up the volume on your energy while you are at a regular horse show, you can set the scene of championships, which are a few months away. As you walk on your horse waiting to compete, you can visualize the venue and environment of championships, imagining you and your horse there, getting ready to go. The energy you create with that visualization is then all set to be channeled into the job at hand.

Ava's Energy Routine

Now when Ava (the irregularly breathing, motivated, and hardworking eventer) goes to an event, she has the following tools in place to adjust her energy. At home when Ava is riding on her own, her mental and physical energy is often low, so she uses this routine to bring her energy up:

- Listening to an upbeat, fun playlist while grooming and tacking up her horse after work

- Imagining the environment of her next competition and visualizing herself walking into the arenas, start box, and in-gate

- Using the motto "Let's get this the first time"—before asking her horse to begin any new part of their work—to create a sense of Positive Pressure (for more on this, see chapter 10)

- Taking three Circle Breaths, done at a more rapid pace, emphasizing the inhale during any walk breaks during her ride

For lessons or shows—when her energy is often up at a 6 or 7—Ava uses these three tools to reduce her energy level so she can get to a 5, her Optimal Energy Zone:

1. Find a quiet place before a cross-country school or jump lesson, or at the show to do Ratio Breathing to relax and clear her mind.

2. Use three Circle Breaths and a short form of the centering visualization to feel grounded and balanced when she first gets on her horse.

3. Channel energy to places in her body that are part of one or two of her performance goals for that ride, such as adding weight to her heels and lengthening her spine.

I keep eating, I keep talking, I laugh. I try to just not make any of it too big a deal, even the Olympic Games. You go there, and yes, it's huge pressure; it's hugely important to not just you but all the thousands of people who are at home and who have do-nated to your team. But in reality it's just another horse show. So I try to just keep everything sort of in that perspective and try to keep myself calm that way.

—Laura Kraut, three-time Olympic show jumper,
Olympic show jumping gold medalist

A TOP TIP

A Circle Breath is like an internal half-halt to get your body and mind powered up appropriately.
Use your energy—don't fear it.

Chapter Highlights
Methods to Adjust Your Energy

✔ Use the Performance-Energy Assessment scale to understand your energy levels.

✔ Get into your Optimal Energy Zone with the use of breathing techniques such as Circle Breathing.

✔ Adjust your energy and focus with centering.

✔ Learn which additional energy adjusters help bring your energy level up or down as needed.

6
Attitude

Positive Beliefs and Self-Talk
Support Your Progress

I MAGINE YOU ARE at your biggest show of the year. On the morning of the first day, you pause to reflect as you put on your boots. You briefly review your last few weeks of preparation as you gather yourself together. You've been working hard at home, riding a lot, and doing your homework. You also went to one show and did quite well. There have been various challenges along the way, but here you are, ready to partner with your horse and give it your best. As you think about the next few days of the show, here are some questions to ponder:

- What do you believe about how you will ride?

- What are you saying to yourself as you finish getting dressed and doing your morning chores?

- What is your overall outlook for the show?

- Do you feel certain your riding will be your best? Why or why not?

- How do you think you'll cope mentally with any difficulties or unexpected situations that crop up?

In this scenario, there are optimal answers. There are ways of thinking that will help you perform, focus, and enact solutions to any horsemanship or riding challenges that come up during the show. The more you believe in yourself, the better you will think, the stronger your attitude will be, and the more consistently you'll be able to put forth your personal best. Optimal patterns of thought are not random or accidental; they are the result of awareness, good habits, and a foundation of self-confidence.

What Do You Believe?

If someone asked you to describe your mental and physical skills as a rider, what would they be? How do you describe yourself? What words and qualities come to mind? Do positive things roll off your tongue, or do doubts and negative judgments jump to the front of your mind?

To begin to explore your belief system, it's helpful to think through some typical scenarios. For example, after a tough day at the barn, do you think about how you put in your best effort and will use what you learned on your next ride? If so, you are exhibiting a terrific attitude and mental strength. If, on the other hand, you have negative thoughts when summarizing the day ("I am such an idiot, and I always lose my focus when _____ happens." Or "I am never going to learn to _____. I am just ruining my horse."), it's probably safe to say your belief system has room for some improvement.

On a day when you have a ride where everything feels amazing, and it's as if you and your horse are positively floating on air, to what do you attribute your success? "Wow, the stars lined up for us today. I can't believe we _____." Or "I wish someone got that on video. I have no idea how that happened." You would probably agree that these responses do not depict very much trust and belief in yourself. Instead, you would ideally have some thoughts after a great ride that reflect a more positive attitude, such as "We are getting better every day at _____. I know I can _____." Or "I trust myself to focus on _____ and ride this well when it really counts; we are going to be great at the horse show."

The Belief Elevator

As you can see in the Belief Elevator below, your beliefs about yourself as a rider are the first floor, underneath your expectations, self-talk, and actions. Your beliefs about yourself as a rider are instrumental in creating your expectations. These expectations then

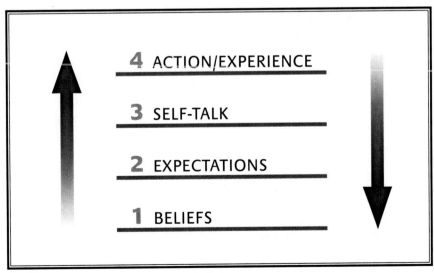

Belief Elevator

contribute to the conversations in your head and shape your ability to act in the moment.

For example, the Belief Elevator may progress up the four floors like this:

1. **Belief.** I ride my best under pressure.

2. **Expectation.** I will be sharp, focused, and effective on my horse today when it matters most.

3. **Self-Talk.** "I am going to nail this ride. I'm excited for this challenge, and I know we can do it."

4. **Action/Experience.** Riding well in the moment and utilizing all my skills and talents to meet the demands of the course, test, or exercise.

The floors can be accessed bottom up and top down. Sometimes experiences and things that happen in your riding have a trickle-down effect in that they impact your self-talk, and then expectations, and then beliefs. For instance, the first time you ever nailed your ride under a lot of pressure, as long as you attributed your success to your effort, skill, and focus, it had an extremely positive impact on your expectations and beliefs about your ability to do it again.

All the floors of the Belief Elevator need to be adjusted as your beliefs take new shape and your successes grow. Be mindful that this process will require both awareness and ongoing maintenance.

In the warm-up I don't want to be thinking whether it's going to be good. I want to get to where I have no doubt in my mind. Like I'll say to myself, "It's not a matter of whether it's going to be good. It's, how good is it going to be?"
—John French, three-time World Champion Hunter Rider,
U.S. show jumping team member

Brainstorming Beliefs

Jane, an upper-level dressage rider, came to me wondering why she didn't believe she could be in the top of her classes at big shows. When she told me about her riding history, she explained that she had made do with a wide variety of horses that came her way while she was growing up because her family had limited resources to contribute to her riding aspirations. Although she had received wonderful instruction, this had led to a great deal of competitive inconsistency all the way up through her mid-twenties.

Now, as a trainer in her early thirties who had some very talented horses, Jane was struggling at some of her biggest competitions. It appeared that our first job was to figure out the full spectrum of her beliefs about herself as a rider, and then adjust them as needed so she could move forward and accomplish her goals.

To fully investigate the beliefs you hold about yourself as a rider, use the Beliefs Brainstorming process (this utilizes the same "clustering" technique you used to create your Motivation Statement).

John French on Kennzo de Coto.

Take out a piece of paper and draw a circle in the middle of it. In the circle, write "I believe I am a rider who . . ." and then ask yourself these questions:

1. What mental skills do I possess that help me ride well?

2. What physical capabilities do I utilize when I ride?

3. Why do I believe I will accomplish my riding goals?

4. What beliefs may be holding me back from being the best rider I can be?

Have each answer coming out of the circle on its own line, much like rays coming out from the sun. This free-form method allows your mind to roam freely, rather than staying in an analytical, listing progression. Let your thoughts surface without judgment; this exercise is for exploration. What do you notice? Are there beliefs you are excited to see? Are there things worth changing?

The positive beliefs you hold that support your skills, effort, and progress are valuable to recognize and highlight. Those beliefs form the foundation of your expectations, self-talk, and actions you will utilize to achieve your goals—they are as valuable as gold, so keep them on display! Write and post them in places where you will run into them occasionally, like giving yourself a gift you can open more than once.

As Jane went through this process, she noticed that she held some beliefs that served her:

- "I am strong and fit; I can ride through any test going for brilliance from start to finish."

- "I bring out the best in any horse I ride."

There were also some beliefs Jane realized were limiting:

- "If I look and act like I am confident at the big shows, people will think I am arrogant."

- "I don't really belong with the top riders."

Jane herself noticed right away that even though she was off to a very good start, she still had some work to do—maybe you do too.

Evaluate Your Beliefs

Your beliefs are something you can adjust, even though when you first uncover them, it may feel as if they're set in stone. Your first job is to sort the quality beliefs from the restrictive ones, and then get the negative beliefs to change or fall away. Acknowledging the positive beliefs as you sort them out will act like a natural fertilizer, and allow them to flourish and blossom. To weed out the limiting beliefs, you must put them through a test to assess if they are rational or irrational, productive or unproductive. Using the questions below will help you with this process. Choose one of your limiting beliefs now and ask yourself the following questions:

1. Is the belief based on objective reality? Would observers see the event the same way I perceive it, or do I exaggerate the situation?

2. Is it useful in some way?

3. Does the belief help me reach my goals, or get in the way?

4. Does the belief create emotions that help me feel empowered and capable while reducing stress?

One of Jane's beliefs was "I don't really belong with the top riders." In this case, when put to the test above, she found the belief to be irrational and unhelpful. It may have felt true to Jane at some point, but it was no longer based in objective reality, as her scores were extremely consistent and she was getting a lot of positive feedback from her peers. Additionally, the belief was not useful in any way; it prevented her from achieving her goals by creating a constant negative expectation, and it made her feel tense, worried, and anxious.

When Beliefs Need Adjusting

Beliefs you hold about yourself as a rider become such an integral part of your internal landscape that you can easily forget they are malleable. Always remember this: Changing your beliefs is possible!

Of course, as you probably expect, it takes more than a simple reversal of thought to make this happen. For example, "I can't remember my courses" to "I remember my courses" is a shift that needs to be grounded in reality, with strategies in place that support its truthfulness. The following are the best ways to promote positive changes in your riding beliefs:

- **Use Post-Ride Notes.** Yet another benefit of tracking your rides with Post-Ride Notes (see chapter 2) is to track progress that will counter your limiting beliefs. Reflecting on and taking note of your successes can be instrumental in shifting your beliefs about certain skills. When you have a negative belief such as "I always get tense and locked up when my horse spooks," you first want to create positive change. Therefore, go to your mental skills toolbox and select some strategies. For example, after the next spook or sudden sideways look by your horse, exhale slowly through your mouth to center yourself and direct both your attention and his toward a specific performance goal. After your ride, record the positive resulting experience in your Post-Ride Notes—no matter how small the improvement may have felt.

Allowing Experience
to Change Your Beliefs

Three-time World Champion Rider John French shares how he
learned to change his thinking:

"[Growing up] I really wanted to do the big shows, but we
didn't have the money for that. I went to the shows with this
15.1-hand Palomino. I was going to the big 'A' shows against
Hunterdon and George Morris's kids. And I was going to these
shows frustrated because I couldn't get anywhere against those
kids and those horses. So I was like, 'I think I'm just going to quit
riding [at shows]. I'll just do it for fun and for pleasure but showing is too discouraging for me.'

"One day my friend said, 'Oh, your picture came out in
the George Morris jumping clinic in *Practical Horseman*.' I had
mailed it to the magazine. George talked about my long hair
and my Palomino horse . . . Then he got to the part about evaluating the rider. The last sentence said, 'All in all, this is the best
example of classic hunter seat equitation I have ever seen.'

"So I thought, 'Well, maybe I can do this.' It changed my
thinking. At sixteen years old, I went and borrowed a friend's
horse. I went by myself and picked it up in the morning and
drove it to the Maryland medal finals—and against everyone
I won. And I was second in the Virginia equitation finals. Then
people started offering me horses to ride and show.

"I had thought, 'I can't do it, I can't do it. I'm not going to
ever beat these kids.' And then, 'You know, maybe if I get some
different horses, and I work a little harder, and get rid of that
negative attitude, maybe I can do it, maybe it will be possible.'"

The Strength of a Positive Attitude

Olympic gold medalist Laura Kraut shares a story that illustrates her ability to put things in perspective under even the most pressure-filled situations, with fantastic results.

"I had a moment in Sydney [Olympics] with the mare Liberty. She was a nine-year-old and basically unproven. On the first day I had to go second, which was OK. And my then husband, Bob, had taken me to the show that morning to ride. I think the class started at 10:00. He was going to get Bobby, our one-and-a-half-year-old, who was with the nanny, and then come back.

"But it was twenty minutes to 10:00 and no Bob. I've already walked the course, I'm riding around, and where are Bob and Bobby? I'm at the Olympics, so this is sort of a big thing.

"Finally, I see him coming up the hill with Bobby and [it turned out] he'd gotten in a car accident. He'd gone the wrong way on a roundabout. But actually in its own way, that was a tension breaker. Here we are [at the Olympics]. Of course you went the wrong way on the roundabout.

"I did laugh. And of course I was relieved. Then I walked up to the ring and the first horse in the ring [had fallen] down and was running around like a wild thing. And my mare was hot. I just looked at my groom, and I just said this is almost comical.

"Then they caught the horse and I had to trot into the ring and it was just so massive. I stopped Liberty and I thought OK, this is it. Then I went on and she was fantastic. I think I was one of only three people to be under the time that day.

"Just talking to my groom about how funny it was [helped me]. That's what I try to do—never let the stress of it get the better of me. I actually try to find humor in most everything."

This process is like looking for a small sliver of sunlight in a room you believed would always be pitch black. No matter how narrow the beam of light, it helps you recognize that light (or in this case, riding confidently through your horse's distractibility) is possible. The more experiences like that you find and record, the more you'll be able to shift your belief system.

- **Watch video.** Another way to create movement in your limiting beliefs is to refute their truthfulness with video evidence. Challenge a belief of "I always round my back in the air over jumps" by reviewing video in which you can see your position on course.

  Watch old video to look for examples of places where you kept your back flat. Also try a new focus tool like using the cue word "Tall" at the base of your jumps while being videotaped at home. You'll then have new evidence (and a new belief as a result) that you are capable of having a flat back in the air!

- **Ask for specific feedback.** Once you have identified and evaluated a belief to be holding you back, you want to go after it in as many ways as possible. Another way to do this is to ask for direct comments about a certain skill. Ask people you respect such as your trainer and good riding friends to give you special feedback on the belief area you want to shift. It is best if you share your motivation with them so they can help you look for examples and experiences from your recent rides to help you counter the negative belief.

When Jane examined her belief about not fitting in with the top riders, she was surprised to find that when she kept Post-Ride Notes for the last few shows, she did, in fact, feel confident riding down the centerline against tough competition. When watching recent video, she could point out multiple strengths, and over time she rebuilt her belief to "I belong and excel in any company."

> [People said], "Oh no, you're not tall enough, you don't have the right build, you don't have enough financial backing." [But] I never listen to "you can't." It's not in my vocabulary. I figure that just means you have to work a little harder at it. That's my idea in general—if you really want to do something badly enough, and you work hard enough at it, then you can achieve almost anything.
> —Margie Engle, Olympic show jumping rider, ten-time AGA Rider of the Year

Attitude and Expectations

Optimistic, positive, upbeat, proactive, assured—all these terms depict a mind-set that creates success and a belief in one's abilities to meet a challenge. As you prepare for a day at the barn or horse show, what sorts of things do you look forward to with respect to your own performance in the saddle? Are you looking forward to accomplishing your goals, or are you worried about difficulties and wondering how things will go?

SELF-EFFICACY

Self-efficacy is a concept that describes an expectation that you can perform a skill successfully. It creates a model that depicts the blend, and at times reciprocal relationship, that occurs between expectations and confidence. You expect to ride well, and you do, so your confidence grows. You feel confident, so your expectations and beliefs are strong, and your riding meets your expectations. Understanding and accepting that your actions directly relate to your accomplishments is a part of having self-efficacy. For example, you believe you can improve your accuracy score on the dressage test through the use of your aids, focus, and half-halts. Or you know you can jump your horse through the tight triple combination by sitting up and keeping your leg at the base of each element. Your self-efficacy has been shown to impact the quality of your performance because it affects how much effort you put into the endeavor and how long you persist when it gets tough.

Research has demonstrated a link between high levels of self-efficacy and sport performance. What this means is that what you expect about your ability to perform well has a consistent impact on your actual rides. How about giving yours a small tune-up? As you prepare for each of your next few rides, be aware of your expectations as you tack up and get ready to get on. Often it is helpful to integrate your performance goals into this equation. By planning to succeed and progress on your goals with specific strategies, you are creating a constructive plan that will direct your expectations, self-talk, and actions.

Positive expectations and recognizing success go a long way in helping you achieve your goals.

Integration of your performance goal strategies into your ride plan shapes your attitude and primes it to be optimistic. Let's say you're targeting leg strength as you get back to riding after taking some time off. You have created strategies for this goal, such as riding for ten minutes without stirrups and doing transitions in two-point both directions of the ring. Therefore, as you tack up your horse for a ride, you are planning for ways to improve and creating an expectation that you'll get stronger.

SOLUTION-ORIENTED ATTITUDE

When challenges come up, riders who immediately begin to look for solutions are demonstrating positive expectations. This solution-oriented attitude is facilitated by two central beliefs: (1) Your response to a challenge is more important than anything else, and (2) you have the skills to meet the challenges you face with your horse. When you employ this orientation, you expect to find solutions and follow this two-step approach when facing a challenge:

1. Acknowledge and accept what is happening, and the reality of the situation.

2. Respond efficiently with your best mental and physical skills.

When you have a solution-oriented attitude, these action steps happen every time there is a challenge, regardless of what it looks like from the outset. Please note that this does not mean that you don't feel any negative emotions or frustration about the situation, but that you do not allow yourself to get stuck in them—particularly when you're in the saddle.

To illustrate this solution-oriented attitude, imagine the following scenario: It is abundantly clear that your horse is having a bad day. He is not in a good mood, to say the least. As you get ready and start to warm up, he is sound, but acting cranky and resistant.

In accordance with Murphy's Law, this is happening on the first day of the clinic you have been looking forward to for months. Thankfully your solution orientation has you briefly acknowledge your disappointment (that the happy, willing horse did not show up to

Strategies to Build Awareness of Your Self-Talk

- **Log.** Track your self-talk by writing down what you can remember saying to yourself before, during, and after a ride. Do this soon after the ride while things are fresh in your mind. Record both positive and negative self-talk. Be particularly curious about what triggers your negative self-talk, how often it happens, and what the content is. This will help you identify times when you can instead focus on solutions and positive, self-supporting reminders.

- **Memory sorting.** Think back through your best and most difficult rides to help you build awareness of self-talk patterns. What do you remember about your self-talk as you got ready, warmed up, rode, and finished? Because these outstanding (on both sides of the equation) rides may be lodged more concretely in your memory bank, they may provide very valuable information.

- **Visualization/video.** Imagine and visualize past rides to tap into your thinking, self-talk, and thoughts. Watching video can facilitate this process because it may trigger deeper and more detailed memories of the ride itself, as well as the preparation and circumstances that may have triggered particular self-talk.

the clinic with you), allow yourself a moment to take a couple of deep breaths to accept the situation as it is, and move swiftly to brainstorming ideas that can help you salvage the day, such as adjusting your goals and channeling any frustration into strength and "oomph" to send him forward.

> *I think the rider's attitude in the ring is transposed to the horse's attitude . . . I think the difference between the good riders and good trips versus the outstanding trips are in large measure the positive attitude and inspiration that one shows to the judge and the way one tackles the problems of the course in riding the horse. I think it's very apparent.*
> —Michael Page, Olympic silver and bronze medalist, three-day eventing

Michael Page on Foster at Badminton in 1968.

Positive Self-Talk

Have you ever seen a rider standing alone near the ring before her ride, nodding her head ever so slightly up and down, with a look of intense concentration on her face? It's a safe bet that part of what that rider is doing is having an internal conversation, engaging in what is known as self-talk. When properly utilized and crafted, this mental skill has the potential to help you be enthusiastic, optimistic, and constructive regarding your performance on your horse. Yes, your thoughts can help you feel better about yourself, your skills, and your approach to riding. When you harness this skill, you have yet another powerful way to funnel deposits into your bank of confidence, which will enhance your performance.

The most common misconception about self-talk is that it has the magical ability to completely transform reality. It's almost as if by your saying the sky is green enough times, the sky will indeed become a bright, emerald green. Or if by telling yourself you are confident when you are scared and shaking in your boots, you will suddenly feel sure of yourself. If you are still holding out hope that this is how self-talk works, please maintain your general optimism but be open to adjusting your core understanding of the skill as you read on.

CHANGING NEGATIVE TO POSITIVE

It would be nice to learn to keep your thoughts 100 percent positive, supportive, and productive all the time. However, this is very difficult and probably not realistic. It is more likely you will have a negative thought every now and again. The key is to not waste your time feeling disappointed when a negative thought crosses your mind. Instead, put your energy toward replacing that thought with a positive, constructive idea.

To practice this, write a list of your most typical negative thoughts. Consider lesson situations, competition scenarios, and any habitual thoughts that are self-defeating. Anything that comes to mind is worth adding to the list. These examples of negative self-talk would be worthy of replacing:

"I can't get my horse light today."

"My mind is going to go blank the second I walk through the in-gate."

"I'll never get a ribbon today—there are so many nice horses here."

"I'm so stupid. I can never remember what my trainer tells me to do."

"I always make mistakes when people are watching."

These prime examples of negative thoughts can interfere with your ability to focus and ride your best. So what do you do? Just flip them around? Do you think that would be effective? It may already be clear to you that a simple black-and-white reversal of these thoughts is not likely to have a big effect—believability is crucial. Use these positive self-talk guidelines to begin to craft your replacements:

1. **Use the present tense.** "I focus" rather than "I will focus."

2. **Utilize powerful language.** Instead of "I ride well," try "I create uphill balance."

3. **Direct your mind and body to solutions.** "I look up and keep my eye on a target."

4. **Remind yourself of skills and talents that feel authentic.** "I am strong and patient; we are well prepared."

As you can see, the replacement needs to contain an active, realistic solution that will help you cope with the specific content of the negative thought. It must be believable and doable in the moment. The replacement should also be straightforward so you can easily imagine the positive thought taking place. Now let's look at suitable positive self-talk replacements for the above negative examples:

☹ "I can't get my horse light today."
☺ "Sending energy to my legs creates forward momentum."

☹ "My mind is going to go blank the second I walk through the in-gate."
☺ "I have a specific plan to direct my focus and stay on task."

☹ "We'll never get a ribbon today—there are so many nice horses here."
☺ "I control my performance; we make a fantastic pair."

☹ "I'm so stupid. I can never remember what my trainer tells me to do."
☺ "I am learning how to break things down into reminders that stay with me."

☹ "I always make mistakes when people are watching."
☺ "I bring my performance goals to the ring every day. I ride for me."

As you saw earlier, your beliefs and expectations play a large role in shaping your self-talk, but remember that the Belief Elevator goes up and down. The self-talk you use can also have an impact on your expectations and beliefs. Positive thinking will trickle down to shape your expectations about future rides, and your belief in your ability to be successful. Again, the most important aspect to assess is whether or not the floors line up in order to get your riding skills where you'd like them. The potential benefits of a positive self-talk statement such as "I am calm and relaxed in the warm-up ring" will not get you very far when it completely counters your belief that "warm-up rings are always scary and dangerous." Stay mindful and aware that the more your self-talk, expectations, and beliefs line up, the better and more consistent your actions will be.

> [My trainers] conditioned us to say things in the positive. If you say you always chip in, then you're going to keep chipping in . . . instead, say what you want: "I always remember to keep the horse in front of my leg." Or "I squeeze the horse off the ground." Turn it around and make yourself say it in the positive.
>
> —Gina Miles, Olympic three-day eventing silver medalist

Gina Miles on McKinlaigh.

THOUGHT STOPPING

Ben came to me worried that he was "ruining" his new horse, Wells. He believed in Wells's talent after seeing him go around beautifully with other riders, but said when he rode the fancy hunter, he "couldn't find his way out of a paper bag."

Ben was inundated with negative fears and doubts when he thought about riding in the division they were targeting this year. The first show on his schedule was fast approaching, so part of what we wanted to do was stop the negative thoughts from stealing so much of his focus. We started by working on the "upper floor" of self-talk, and then made our way down to expectations and beliefs after he got some good experiences under his belt.

To enable Ben to take more control of his thoughts, we crafted a negative thought-stopping cue; this would be his default response every time he had a negative thought. A thought-stopping cue is a word, short phrase, image, or physical reminder that you use to silence the internal negative voice. Once the negative thought has been quieted, you have the opportunity to replace it with a constructive, solution-oriented idea.

Part of what makes negative self-talk statements so vicious is that they encourage you to enter into dialogue centered on poisonous (and often simply untrue) content. For example, Ben would get stuck scolding himself in lessons after a small mistake, and this would in turn distract him and ruin his attitude. The thought-stopping cue was something he could use just like a clutch to shift gears in the moment, allowing him to regroup and choose a new track.

Creativity and personal relevance are crucial for thought-stopping cues to be effective. Here are some types of cues and specific examples:

- Words
  - Serious: "Stop," "Delete"

- ❏ Process-oriented: "Breathe," "Focus"

- ❏ Silly: "Fudgesicle," "Kapow"

- Short phrases

  - ❏ "Moving on"

  - ❏ "Let it go"

- Images

  - ❏ A white board full of negative thoughts being erased

  - ❏ A giant red stop sign

- Physical reminders

  - ❏ Shrugging your shoulders up toward your ears, and then rolling them back and down

  - ❏ Slowly exhaling through your mouth

  - ❏ Looking up toward the sky and then focusing on a target in front of you

Ben decided that he wanted to use the phrase "Go forward!" as his thought-stopping cue because it prompted him to move past his negativity and doubled as a reminder for what he needed to do in the ring. This cue became his first response to a negative thought, and his method for getting control back over his attention so he could change gears and craft a positive response. When he said "I can't find my way out of a paper bag" to himself at the show, he immediately said "Go forward!" and created the response "I count to keep our rhythm. Wells is on my team."

I point out something good about every round and discuss it with them. I'm very conscious of trying not to use the word "don't" or "not." I try to replace it with how to do it right. I

*usually think it through before I talk to the kids. Instead of say-
ing "Don't use a pulley rein," I would probably say, "It would
be a lot more effective if you use a direct rein." I try to phrase
my responses to the kids in a way that I'm not just showing
them what they did wrong, but making sure that they understand what the correction is.*

—Stacia Madden, top hunter/jumper/equitation trainer

Affirmations

The character Stuart Smalley, of *Saturday Night Live* fame, repeated
this classic affirmation in the mirror: "I'm good enough, I'm smart
enough, and doggone it, people *like* me." Although this skit and
character poked fun at affirmations, it also modeled supporting one-
self with positive self-talk. Sort of like watching someone drink a
glass of milk with a silly straw, you saw that affirmations could be
enjoyable and good for you!

Have you ever reminded yourself of your strengths and skills while
you were facing a challenge? For example, while walking into the
start box, have you thought, "We can do this!"? Or have you smiled
as you went through the in-gate and said to yourself, "I have a great
plan and we are going to rock!"? If so, terrific! These informal affirmations mobilized your strengths as part of your preparation. There's
also value to be gained from the more formalized process of crafting
the affirmations and then using them at preplanned strategic times.

An affirmation is a positive self-statement that describes what
you want in yourself. Skills, physical abilities, mental strengths, beliefs, attitudes, and the relationship you have with you horse—all
can be supported by powerfully worded reminders of what you want
to enjoy in your riding.

When you write affirmations, you're using a form of positive
self-talk to build your positive beliefs about yourself. If the beliefs

Powerful affirmations are based on your successes and accomplishments.

are just forming, perhaps occurring to you as part of your dreams and goals about becoming the best rider you can be, you are strengthening them each time you shape them into useable self-statements. Brainstorming, creating, editing, and turning affirmations over in your mind helps you color in the vision of yourself as a rider who possesses those very skills.

Examine your performance goals and Post-Ride Notes to find the best subject matter for your affirmations. Goals you believe you are making progress on are a fantastic starting place, as are highlights and accomplishments from previous rides. Looking in these places for ideas will assist you in choosing things you truly feel good about, areas of your riding that you honestly take pride in and want to continue to develop.

When you're crafting an affirmation, keep the following in mind:

- It is an "I" statement.

- It is written in the present tense.

- It has powerful wording.

- It is positive.

- It does NOT have a *should, would, could, can, want,* or *if*.

Here are a few good examples:

- "I am focused."

- "I ride forward out of the corner."

- "I thrive and ride my best in high-pressure situations."

- "I am confident in my preparation; my horse and I trust each other."

And here are a few guidelines for how, when, and where to use your affirmations:

1. Say your affirmations to yourself before or during your rides to boost your confidence and direct your focus. This can be aloud when appropriate (such as when driving to the barn), or in your mind (as you walk around the ring before you start schooling your horse).

2. Visualize the end product as you say your affirmation. For example, what do you look and feel like when you're riding with trust in your horse? Or riding with confidence to the big, square oxer? See and feel those types of specific pictures in your mind that represent the manifestation of your affirmations.

3. Write your affirmations on small index cards or Post-its, and place them in strategic spots (in your tack trunk, coat bag, on a mirror, on your cell phone). Say them, either aloud or to yourself, when you read the card.

4. You can employ affirmations as an antidote to help reverse negative thoughts and statements. Do this by saying an opposing affirmation several times after a negative thought has been halted with a thought-stopping cue.

A TOP TIP

Belief in your own skill causes accomplishments
to happen—if you build it, they will come.

Chapter Highlights
Ways to Maintain a Positive Attitude

✔ Assess and adjust your beliefs about your skills in order to support your progress.

✔ Maintain a solution-oriented attitude when facing a challenge.

✔ Use the positive self-talk strategies of changing negatives to positives, thought-stopping cues, and affirmations to create an optimistic, can-do attitude.

7

Preparation

Build a Preparation Routine
to Increase Consistency

EQUESTRIANS HAVE DIFFERENT ways they get comfortable and into their groove before a ride. Some may polish their boots to a high gloss while listening to their iPod, while others may sit quietly on a tack trunk, drinking some water and thinking about their plan. How about you? Are there things you do before you get on that help you clear your mind of distractions and focus on creating a great ride? Go ahead; give yourself a moment to think about it.

What comes to mind? Do you have a good list? Is it hard to think of anything? Is it completely different at home versus at a show, before a lesson versus prior to a school by yourself? "It depends"? You know some things that help, but don't always make time for them?

How about this question: Do you know your horse's preparation routine? Most likely the answer is yes. You may have basics that you adapt depending on the circumstances of the day, but tried-and-true preparation methods are probably easy to remember. What accounts

Mental preparation can occur during regular chores.

for the fact that it is often easier to stick to your horse's routine than your own? Well, obviously, horses can't do it for themselves, so you as a rider are inherently predisposed to help them. Additionally, the culture of equestrian sport can make you forget that you are an athlete who has specific preparation needs too.

Remember, there are two players on your team—you and your horse, and you *both* need quality preparation to perform well. This means that you know exactly what preparation will help you peak, focus, and excel in the moment when it counts. The recipe is simple: Self-awareness about preparation factors that help you, plus a measure of the appropriate mental skills, will create a regular pre-ride routine that can increase your consistency and confidence on your horse.

I always make sure I get a good night's sleep. I don't go out late the night before. I don't eat a big dinner. I usually like to have a routine. . . Near the competition, I have a normal time of breakfast, go to the barn, go for a walk with the horses—not just sit around twiddling my thumbs until the competition. I keep myself occupied. I don't want to sit down and just start thinking about it and then get myself all worked up hours and hours beforehand. So I keep myself busy in a positive way.

—Guenter Seidel, three-time Olympic

dressage bronze medalist

Examine Your Best Recent Rides

Have you ever had a day when it felt like lightning struck, and you and your horse were brilliant together? What do you think happened? What made that day so terrific? Is it hard to figure out? Sometimes these rides feel amazing, but the factors that created them are a real mystery. Instead of shaking your head and saying "I really don't know, but I hope it happens again soon," stay curious and determined to figure it out. Your goal is not to overanalyze the intangible magic that can occur between you and your horse, which may well be part of what you love about the sport, but to discover clues that contribute to your best rides so you can create them more often.

To play the role of the detective in this case, pick out three of your best rides from the last few months. They can be from a lesson, a schooling session on your own, or competition. These rides need not be entirely and utterly fantastic from start to finish, but they must stand out in your mind as times when you and your horse achieved excellence, partnership, and true harmony. Take a few minutes to write this down:

- Where and when the ride happened

- Any details you remember about the situation, environment, and the ride itself

Next, rewind the memory even further to examine that experience in its entirety, and the events leading up to your ride. Anything that stands out in your memory from earlier that day, the hour or two before the ride, or immediately prior to getting on your horse can be valuable. Now write this down:

- What you remember about your focus, self-talk, and attitude

- Anything you did to physically prepare for your ride (stretching, nutrition/hydration, exercise)

- Actions you took to create your environment or adjust your energy (music, conversation with others or your horse, where you spent your time)

Some of what you remember may be seemingly random factors that were out of your control, like a certain song coming on the radio in the car or your trainer telling a joke as you walked out of the warm-up ring. These are useful too, so take note of all of them; you can replicate what's in your control and approximate what isn't.

As you look at the preparation factors for these best rides, you may start to see themes and items that come up more than once. If so, smile and say "Bingo!"—it means you're on the right track. Let's say you notice that some of the rides occurred when you had time to yourself to think and review your goals for the day before you got on—this is terrific because it is something you can build into your routine on a consistent basis. To be certain you make that happen, create a separate list of the items or themes you notice in this process so you can be sure to put them into your regular routine. A productive list might include items like these:

- Mentally review my performance goals for the day's ride.

- Switch my focus with a cue word each time I get stuck on something outside my control (such as the weather or another person's opinion).

- Use Circle Breathing to adjust my energy.

- Listen to fun music to foster an upbeat, optimistic attitude.

I remember walking to the in-gate at the Olympic Games in Los Angeles and thinking, "Wow, this is it," and I remember coming out and thinking, "Oh, that was a blast and so much fun." I didn't even think about being nervous because when you're

prepared and you know you have crossed every "t" and dotted
every "i," you have a confidence that trumps nerves and allows
you to feel excitement while you enjoy the ride!
—Melanie Smith Taylor, Olympic show jumping
gold medalist

General Preparation Components

Hopefully you just recognized that you already do some terrific things to prepare to get on your horse (if not, have no fear, as there are many valuable ideas to come). The odds are also very high that in your non-horsey, day-to-day life, you have interests and cross-training routines that add to your abilities. It is key to recognize how, what, and why those factors are contributing to your riding readiness. Why?

Understanding what enables you to ride beautifully helps ground your confidence in specific, tangible practices that you trust. As you read on, you may become motivated to add breadth to your general preparation methods, or renew your commitment to what has been valuable to you in the past.

Pamela was an eventing client, competing two horses and moving them both up to new divisions when she decided to fine-tune her mental skills. It was clear from the beginning that what she did to support her riding skills away from the barn was already exemplary. She cross-trained with running and Pilates, was extremely organized with her equipment and horse management, and was very disciplined about her energy and rest practices.

Pamela and I acknowledged her competence in her general preparation and talked about how it served her. As we identified all the modalities she utilized, it was exciting to see her renewed faith and commitment to her regular process. Factors she had dialed in included some of the following:

Use Life Skills as Preparation Factors

Adapting mental skills from other areas of your life that can prepare you to ride well is like bringing your horse a pie you baked from apples off the big apple tree in your backyard. You've got a ton of apples—why not use them and bring the tasty results to the barn? The following life skills can be valuable to include when you prepare to ride at home or in competition.

- **Job skills.** Think about your job—do you employ things like focus, tenacity, and a can-do attitude? Could those be useful to you in the saddle? Instead of thinking you have to have a separate skill set, make a list of your workplace skills you can use in your riding.

- **Organization/time management.** Let's say you are capable of being on time to work, meeting deadlines, tracking your weekly goals and responsibilities, and keeping your refrigerator stocked. Many of those types of management skills can be applied toward effectively preparing you, your horse, your equipment, and your riding calendar.

- **School.** How do you get confident to take an exam? What makes you understand a confusing topic? How do you stick to a homework routine? The mental skills that help you learn, succeed, and navigate your education are applicable in an equestrian setting where learning and growth are a large part of being the best rider you can be.

- **Coping skills.** The water line under the kitchen sink just sprang a big leak. What do you do? What qualities do you have that help you cope with the unexpected? Are you levelheaded? Rational? Calm under pressure? Able to ask the right people for help? Remember that the best of who you are is always with you, available to help you deal with the unexpected ups and downs of equestrian sport.

- **Relationship/communication.** Your ability to support your friends, share the things that are important to you, and be honest and genuine when you communicate can facilitate a terrific working relationship with your trainer and, most importantly, your horse.

- **Other sports.** What other sports have you played in your life? What mental skills did you employ? Often these skills get lost in translation when you walk into the barn, and instead they should be front and center. Reminding yourself of the qualities and talents you've used in other athletic settings is a wonderful way to boost your confidence and feel more prepared to meet your riding challenges.

- **Physical cross-training.** Riding is very physically challenging, a fact that is not lost on the rider who is looking to excel. It is widely accepted that fitness and strength will increase proficiency in equestrian sport. It is also important to note that it is easy for a lack of physical conditioning and cardio strength to translate into nerves or anxiety. When your heart rate gets elevated, your breathing quickens and you may go into oxygen debt. Your mind can experience this as extreme stress and prompt your body to sound the alarm bells. You then have a mental and physical challenge to overcome.

Supporting yourself with a blend of cardiovascular and

strength training, balance work, stretching, core training, and/ or complimentary sports will have a significant impact on your overall riding abilities. Finding qualified professionals in those areas to help you tailor cross-training to fit into your schedule and meet your needs is ideal. Books, DVDs and online training can also give you ideas and inspiration to create your own methods and practices. It can be useful to have a variety of routines, some for when you have a lot of time, and others for days when your schedule is packed.

I recommend my riders go to the gym. I try to go as well . . . your fitness is such a big part of it . . . you're also trying to eat sensibly, as much as anybody can. I feel if you're strong and toned and healthy, then your performance, like in any sport, is going to be enhanced.
    —Missy Clark, top hunter/jumper/equitation trainer

- **Ongoing physical maintenance.** Massage, chiropractic, acupuncture/acupressure, sport medicine, and physical therapy aren't just for your horse (hopefully that is not a surprise!). Your body's physical health will directly affect not only your ability to use your aids in the saddle, but your focus, attitude, and energy level as well. Imagine managing a painful knot in your back while trying to tack up, maintain a positive attitude, and create straightness and impulsion with your horse during your lesson—not easy!

  An open mind will help you honestly assess your physical health, along with creating a willingness to seek out the assistance of licensed professionals. Keep your long-term calendar in mind to schedule regular maintenance appointments and effectively plan around your competition schedule.

- **Rest.** Surprised? You may think you were born knowing how to rest and so do not need to pay any special attention to this factor. Not the case! True mental and physical rest is necessary to adequately recharge your batteries. Prioritizing rest in your day-to-day life is an indispensable way to guarantee you will have mental strength when you need it most.

  What qualifies as rest? Examples include getting enough hours of sleep; taking clear, mental breaks from things like multitasking and electronic media to think about riding; closing your eyes and/or putting your feet up for even brief periods throughout your normal day (even a minute or two can make a difference); creating a private micro-environment like your car or tack room to have a quiet moment to yourself.

- **Nutrition.** Would you ever skip giving your horse breakfast? Or suddenly change what he ate? Your horse has an optimal nutrition routine and you do as well. As with so many of the skills in this book, knowing yourself and how you operate best is essential. What, when, how, and where you eat and drink in order to care for yourself as an athlete starts with using this self-knowledge and good, old-fashioned common sense. For example, you can't race a car that has no gas, and the engine will knock and ping if you use the wrong kind.

  Be prepared to support yourself nutritionally by bringing things to the barn or horse show that you know and trust to work for you and your body. Educate yourself or work with a nutritionist to develop an optimal nutrition routine, and then commit to being consistent and disciplined about this part of your preparation.

  I do drink a lot of Propel and Gatorade and water. I have a big

mug I keep with me all day long [with] ice in it . . . I drink a lot
of fluids all day long [to] keep from getting dehydrated.
—Margie Engle, Olympic show jumping rider,
ten-time AGA Rider of the Year

See anything here that you want to add to your general preparation? If so, try to pick out two new methods to do in the coming
week, put them on your calendar, and get them done—the positive
changes you will feel will motivate and invigorate you.

Superstition and Good-Luck Rituals

Superstitions and good-luck rituals can be defined as parts of
your routine that do not have inherent or objectively identified benefits attached. You put on your left boot first, align
your bracelets so they all face the same way, kiss your horse on
the nose before you walk him to the mounting block, wear blue
socks or lucky socks or the socks your grandmother gave you or
the same socks all week during championships, and it makes you
feel terrific? Great! Generally speaking, as long as you're doing
something simple within your control, these rituals are fine (not
necessarily encouraged, but fine).

The time to be careful is when your good-luck ritual starts
to impinge on other parts of your routine that are necessary
and essential for your preparation, or your superstitions center
on things out of your control. If touching *each* of your horse's
braids as you tack up slows you down and makes you late to the
ring, or if you're worried because your favorite song didn't "happen to" play on the radio, it may be time to make some changes.

Pre-Ride Routines

If you're like a lot of people, you regularly do some experimenting in the kitchen when cooking a meal—a little of this and a pinch of that. Sometimes you are just trying to get by with what's in your house to avoid going to the grocery store. Your basic cooking skills are always in place, but the preparation, inspiration, and ingredients may vary. Once you have enjoyed the meal, it is so easy to forget what went into it. You may have even created some of your most amazing dishes in the last few months and wish you could make them again—for the big party you're having next week, for example. Wouldn't it give you confidence to know the ingredients you'll need instead of simply hoping it will all come together? How would it feel to be able to trust that you have a routine and method to cook the very meal that will knock your guests' socks off?

A pre-ride routine is a lot like having a tried-and-true recipe, but it is a recipe for success. It is also a very personal recipe because you created it. You build a quality pre-ride routine by keeping track of the mental preparation strategies from your best rides, practicing excellent general long-term preparation strategies, and then having specific methods in place that get you thinking, feeling, and riding your best.

The description and timing of a pre-ride routine can vary. It is described here as mental preparation and management strategies that you use up to an hour or two before a ride. This is not to say that the entire time must be spent on the routine, or that the components must always happen in a particular order. These mental skills can blend seamlessly into your regular horse preparation and responsibilities. The goal is to find components you believe in and tailor them to fit your style.

I hope you discovered some of your favorite preparation factors when you examined your best recent rides, so be sure to include them in your pre-ride routine. What else should be a part of it? Well, the fact is, no one can tell you—it's best to educate yourself with ideas, then experiment, review your best rides, and be creative. The best riders in the world will tell you that they never stop learning about being excellent horse people, and the same is true of learning about yourself to uncover your best. As you look through some of the ideas presented here, take note of things that interest you intuitively. Try them out and see what sticks.

Having consistency in your preparation is key for your focus.
—Bernie Traurig, rider, clinician, Founder/President,
Equestriancoach.com

Pre-Ride Routine Ingredients

Although all mental skills can be appropriate to include in a pre-ride routine, being judicious with your mental energy is also essential. Take what you know about how you prepare best, add some new ingredients, and then choose carefully so your pre-ride recipe is not too long. Here are some ideas to consider:

VISUALIZATION

Using your mind's eye to generate the feel and experiences you want with your horse will instill focus, as well as help your physical and mental abilities be more accessible while you ride.

- **At your barn.** The content of your visualization at your own barn will vary based on what you're working toward. A brief, simple visualization of your schooling plans and performance goals coming to fruition will prepare your mind and body to be successful. Each time you picture a certain movement or aid, you will be building muscle memory and increasing the likelihood that it will happen in reality with the same quality you imagine. If crisp walk/canter transitions are your goal, visualize two or three of them happening successfully.

When you're preparing for a particular competition, it's helpful to visualize the venue and the mental strength you want at the show. This type of visualization can also serve to raise your energy level for the lesson or schooling ride that day if needed. Or it can give you an opportunity to practice lowering your arousal level with your best energy adjusters if just thinking about the show increases your heart rate.

Visualization can also direct your emotional intentions as you visualize and create your ride in your mind's eye. To highlight this benefit, imagine a section of your ride and concentrate on feeling a particular emotion, such as patience, calm, clarity, confidence or motivation with your horse that day.

- **At a show.** The visualization you do at the show will be a crucial component of your mental preparation. Use the time before your ride to observe your ring, arena, or course so you can add detail and vividness to the visualization. Because your ride or course plan is ideally set before you visualize, you can include how your performance goals and strategies will allow you to be successful. Within a pre-ride routine, less is more with regard to visualization. Better to go through your ride once at high quality instead of many times quickly or incompletely to avoid causing mental fatigue and undermining your focus.

[At a big competition], I would go to the ring at some point during the day and I'd try to find a quiet time. I would sit behind the ring and shut my eyes. Then I'd open them up and I would literally ride what I felt would be the entire test, almost every footfall. And knowing where there might be issues with a particular movement, I'd think about the specific preparation

coming into it. I really would break it all down and I'd go over it step-by-step. I felt that when I got in there, I was much more prepared because of that.

—Debbie McDonald, Olympic dressage bronze medalist, first U.S. World Cup Dressage champion

Debbie McDonald on Brentina at the 2005 World Cup Finals.

Sample Pre-Ride Routines

At Home

1. Take three Circle Breaths before getting out of your car to transition from work to riding, recover from the commute, and adjust your energy to an optimal level.

2. While getting your horse out, look at the ring or arena to assess the new environment for that day's lesson.

3. As you groom your horse, notice his mood and make your

connection for the day. Use verbal and nonverbal communication to establish your working relationship.

4. Think about two performance goals to integrate into that day's ride, such as staying tall in the air over the jumps and keeping your fingers closed on the reins.

5. Stretch lightly in the tack room before putting on your horse's bridle.

6. On the mounting block, use the cue word "Harmony" to transition from planning and preparing to actually riding with feel and instinct.

At a Show

1. Eat a snack of a banana and electrolyte water to keep your nutrition and hydration on track.

2. Facilitate your connection with your horse and warm up your body by taking your horse out for a hand-walk while reviewing your goals for the day.

3. Go up to the ring to learn and assess the course, ring, schedule, and conditions.

4. Find a place to visualize your ride plan.

5. As you stretch your hamstrings, calves, and back, listen to a fun music playlist to channel your energy productively and warm up your mind-body connection.

6. Use the affirmation "I am prepared to be effective and ride our plan" to direct your focus to your own performance as you walk toward the warm-up ring.

Energy Management

It is wise to have a routine that helps you be aware of your energy level before you ride. You can then make adjustments *before* putting your horse's energy level into the equation.

- *Energy-assessment breath:* Choose a moment within your preparation time, such as before you get out of the car at the barn, while putting on your boots, or while getting your equipment ready, to take a Circle Breath and assess your energy level. Is it a little too high? A bit flat and blah? Just right?

- *To lower your energy level:* To relax, focus on an extra slow, gentle exhale through your mouth. With this exhale, relax and let go of any tension you feel, particularly in the specific muscles that typically get tight and stiff.

Michelle Spadone prepares herself at the back gate.

- *To increase your energy level:* Lift your chin, open your chest, fix your gaze on one particular point ahead of you, and take a few strong breaths with an increased pace. Picture yourself breathing in the elements of strength and power to store for later use.

ASSESSMENT/ANALYSIS

As you start to interact with your horse, what do you notice about his mood? What's the weather like today? Is there a new course in the ring for your lesson? Set aside times to assess each factor that will impact your ride on a given day. Once you have assessed, for example, that it is windy and cold at the barn, and your horse is feeling fresh, you can analyze the situation, time, and resources you have and choose the right skills to respond accordingly.

RIDE PLAN

Creating a thorough ride plan, perhaps with the help of your trainer, is a way to bring excellence and consistency to your rides. A ride plan contains not just the "what" of the ride, but also the "how." Your performance goals are valuable pieces to add into the ride plan, as they are specific ways to harness your focus appropriately for what you and your horse are working on. When incorporated within a pre-ride routine, the process of creating a ride plan may differ greatly if you are schooling or competing because of the information and time available.

- **At home.** When you're schooling or in a lesson, the ride plan can happen in two parts. The first step is to review your performance goals and strategies before you get on. For instance, you remind yourself of your strategy to use the cue word "Melt" as you canter into each corner during your flatwork to help you relax your back and seat.

   Second, although not technically part of the pre-ride timeline, you integrate the same strategy before executing a specific exercise during your ride. So continuing with our example, take a moment while at the halt or walk to imagine yourself saying and feeling the cue word "Melt" in each corner before you begin your left-lead canter work.

- **At a show.** When you are competing, you often have more time to build a ride plan because you know your test or course before you mount up. Give yourself some time to create the plan. Go over it in your mind, write or draw it out, and visualize it once to help you remember it thoroughly.

RIDER WARM-UP

Warming up your own body before you get on your horse can be extremely useful. It will help you find your center and balance, enable your muscles to more effectively activate on cue, and get you to feel more present in the moment. Having methods and strategies to accomplish this within your pre-ride routine may take some creativity.

There may be times when something like light physical activity (such as a short, brisk walk) before getting your horse ready can loosen you up. Modifying pieces of the cross-training you already do in your normal general preparation is a terrific way to generate ideas. Also useful can be stretching or yoga—there are many books and skilled professionals dedicated to helping riders integrate those types of skills into their pre-ride routine.

INTROSPECTION

Think of this as time alone to sit and gather yourself. It can help you get focused on your plan, allow you to feel comfortable and composed, and give you a chance to take a break from socializing or task-related activities. This may be facilitated by finding a place to sit down alone such as in your car, a quiet tack room, or under a tree. Or put headphones on—with or without music—to create a small "bubble" around you.

HORSE CONNECTION

Do you have a conversation with your horse as you put on his halter? Do you take time to pick the hay out of his mane and forelock before you take him out of the stall? The time you take on the ground to groom, tack up, communicate with, and generally spend time with your horse is invaluable. It builds trust and creates a bond that you build during your riding time. The moments you spend with him may take many different shapes depending on the day, but it is important to acknowledge that your quality time together can be a key step in your pre-ride preparation routine.

TRANSITION CUE

A transition cue is your reminder to "get out of your head" and into your body to ride your horse with trust, instinct, and feel. This aspect of your pre-ride routine is an important one, since it enables a shift from the more mental tasks of assessment, analysis, planning, verbal communication, and visualization to physical skills and the quality mind-body connection required for riding.

A transition cue should happen very close to the time when you get on your horse. It may be saying a phrase like "We are prepared" to yourself as you walk your horse out of the cross-ties, or taking two breaths on the mounting block before you put your foot in the stirrup.

By having a transition cue, you make a conscious decision to leave all your preparation and pre-ride strategies behind you, and go forward with your focus firmly anchored in the moment and a positive attitude.

Keep things fresh by modifying some of your pre-ride routine strategies on a regular basis. For example, if you use music to adjust your energy level, try creating a fresh playlist every couple of weeks to increase your energy as you tack up at home.

On the day [of a big class], I have to have plenty of time to rest in the afternoon . . . do some yoga. I can't be rushed. That's one thing I know about myself—in order to get into this, I have to have time to do all my weird things that I do.
—John French, three-time World Champion Hunter Rider,
U.S. show jumping team member

A TOP TIP

Prepare to succeed—or leave the quality
of your ride to chance.

Chapter Highlights
Preparation Techniques

✔ Examine your best recent rides to identify valuable preparation elements.

✔ Refine basic preparation components such as rest, cross-training, and nutrition.

✔ Carefully build a pre-ride routine for use at home and at shows. Include items like visualization, energy management, rider warm-ups, and transition cues.

8
Communication

Communicate Effectively to
Develop Teamwork and Trust

A TEENAGER NAMED TALIA sits on her horse waiting for her lesson to start. She is eager to work on a few specific things she has been having trouble with and wants to ask her trainer about her new saddle pad. As she waits, Talia's reins are held loosely in one hand, and she's slumped with comfort in the saddle, her heels up with her feet lightly connected to the stirrups. She is trying to daydream about her upcoming show but feels distracted by a conversation she had with her mom on the way to the barn.

When Talia's trainer gets to the ring and asks if she is ready, she says "Yes!" but her trainer, noting her posture and horse's half-closed eyes, remains unconvinced (as does her horse, who proceeds to take much urging and kicking to move forward into anything resembling a working trot). The lesson has not started off on a particularly good note; there is confusion and mixed messages flying around the ring, and it will be a toss-up as to whether anyone's efforts (rider, trainer, or horse) lead to good things.

Although equestrian disciplines are referred to as individual sports, anyone who has ever had the good fortune to sit on a horse knows that's not quite accurate. Your horse is your teammate; there are no two ways about it. Your team also includes your trainer and supporters who all contribute immeasurably to your success. Riding is an endeavor that requires constant communication with those around you.

In this example, the teenager was communicating—the trouble was that the messages she was conveying verbally and nonverbally were not harmonious. Although this is far from unusual or unique, it is remarkable how with just a little awareness and attention, communication can be improved to a point where everyone works more effectively as a team. In fact, in all my years as a mental skills coach teaching riders sport psychology techniques to better their preparation and performance practices, I have only once been contacted by someone whose priority was to improve her communication skills and relationships with people on her team. Interestingly, however, it almost always ends up getting discussed when I help people add and organize the skills in their mental toolbox.

Even though it is not something many people think about overtly, quality communication (or lack thereof) affects more riders in more ways on a daily basis than they realize. How you communicate—a skill that includes listening, by the way—is an essential part of accessing your best talents, instincts, and abilities because it ensures that time and energy are not being wasted in translation or misunderstandings, and everyone's efforts are directed to the same place. When communication is clear and your message is received seamlessly, think how much more effective you can be on a given task. Ignoring communication problems can be like trying to run a race even though you know one of your sneakers is untied. Distracted, you are going to run at an irregular pace and may trip and fall down before you cross the finish line. This doesn't sound like a good idea or a good time, wouldn't you agree?

Can you think of some times in the recent past when you have been pleased with your communication at the barn? Perhaps it was a great conversation with your trainer after a lesson? Or feeling your horse eager and willing to partner with you on a difficult movement? Talking with your family about how you appreciated their support at your last show? These instances are important to recognize because looking for exemplary moments will increase their significance and improve the likelihood that you will create them again. Too often, communication is addressed only after there has been a breakdown or a problem, and I strongly recommend to instead be proactive about this skill. Understand how your interactions affect those on your team, and fine-tune your communication skills to improve your preparation and performance.

Communication as a Skill

In a magical fantasy world, people around you would read your mind, anticipate your needs, and dedicate themselves to understanding your perspective. It's not clear who lives on that planet; I have certainly not met anyone from there, have you? Instead, I hear statements like these:

- "I really don't think she understands where I'm coming from."

- "There is one person at the barn who is so hard to be around, and I can't figure out how to handle it."

- "Nobody gets how important riding is to me."

- "I don't think my horse believes me when I tell him to go forward."

Remember at the start of this book when you asked yourself what you wanted to create with your riding, and examined your motivation and desire to be the best rider you could be? Statements like the ones above can prevent you from accessing your best abilities. Why? Because it takes a team effort to get you where you want to go. In addition, those statements are examples of beliefs that keep you stuck in habits that limit your abilities.

Improving in sport, as with anything, requires always being open to learning new things that will help make you better. So when I hear those types of negative comments from riders about their communication, I am always quick to remind them that the past, along with their personality tendencies and habits, does not define them. Do you want to improve? Really? Then you need to be willing to adapt and grow not only as an individual but also as a team member. So if I hear "Oh, I'm not good at speaking up. My trainer misunderstands me a lot," I immediately perceive that as yet another opportunity to build skill—in this case, the ability to communicate effectively.

A good place to start is to think about what you like and appreciate when others are communicating with you. Do you notice when someone says "Great, looking forward to seeing you tomorrow," but it's said quickly, in a flat tone, with a serious face? How does it make you feel? Happy? Worried? Optimistic? Confused? Ideally, you treat others as you wish to be treated. Do you relish getting mixed messages? Probably not, and if you really think about what you appreciate in how others communicate with you, the fundamentals of being clear and genuine come to the surface quickly.

You need to find a system for each person that works for them. [Some riders] need space. When they come out of the ring and they didn't ride well, they know they didn't ride well . . . Those kinds of kids I can just look at, they know that I care, and I just let them go their way. And maybe an hour or so later, or maybe that night, or maybe the next day, then we talk about it. But there are times to talk and there are times to just let it go.

—Susan Hutchison, U.S. show jumping team member

Communicating Effectively

If you think through your most important relationships with regard to your riding and realize you'd like to improve them, having new ideas at your disposal will help. Here are several to consider:

- **Be direct and straightforward.** The simpler your language, the easier it is for your listener to understand. Which of the following would be easier for your trainer to respond to? "When I try to get a more active trot, he goes, 'I'm tired, I don't want to.' And then I get super tired trying to go forward all the way around the ring—and I hate to nag him!" Or "He's lazy today—I think I should carry a crop, OK?"

- **Think through important or challenging subjects beforehand.** Give your message plenty of thought and focus on making it concise. When you need to talk about a difficult subject, consider practicing what you'll say or writing it down first. You can then edit your points for clarity and length, which will greatly improve the odds that you'll be understood.

- **Use active listening whenever you can.** Paraphrase, ask clarifying questions, and acknowledge and accept the other person's viewpoint as valid. Imagine you just listened to all your husband's concerns about your leaving your four-year-old son (and husband, dog, and cat) for the weekend to go to a show five hours away, and you said, "I really get it that you are worried and you feel stressed. What can I do to help you feel better?" Do you think your husband would feel heard and supported? Yes!

- **Use "I" statements.** Own your message with "I" statements when you want to communicate your feelings on a difficult subject: "I'm worried I haven't ridden enough to stay focused and be consistent at the clinic." This engages your listener in helping you face a challenge, instead of hearing you stay stuck in negativity and hitting a brick wall with a statement like this: "We won't do well this weekend—the auditors and the crazy traffic at that facility will be so distracting."

- **Stick to one issue.** When starting a new discussion about something that is important to you, try to stick to one subject at a time. Too much information or too many main points will convolute your message, making it even more difficult for someone to help you mobilize your strengths.

- **Line up your nonverbal messages with your verbal ones.** Appearance, posture, gestures, body position, facial expression, and voice quality (pitch, tempo, rhythm) are all things that communicate your true feelings and intent as you share your views with those around you. You build trust with your listeners by being mindful to match what you say with how you say it. "We're ready" said to your trainer before you go into the competition arena with a smile and a nod, shoulders back, and chest open will convey your authentic confidence.

- **Explain the "why" that underlies the message right away.** This will enable your listeners to access their empathetic response, while providing clarity about your feelings. Explain your behavior or choices from the get-go to show your genuine desire to connect with the recipient of your message. "I'm not jumping today" leaves your trainer full of worry and with a lot of unanswered questions. Prevent the worry and disconnected moment by instead saying initially, "I didn't get any sleep last night and think I would do best to just work on the flat today."

- **Have empathy for those around you.** Expressing compassion will set a tone of understanding and acceptance. Showing that you feel for someone's personal experience and that you value his or her contribution to the team helps the team run smoothly. "I understand it must be hard to teach all day without a break. Is there anything I can do to help you?"

- **Choose and schedule good times to talk.** Demonstrate your respect and positive intentions by asking for someone's attention at an appropriate moment. For example, Saturday morning at the barn, when lessons are in full swing, is probably not an ideal time to talk to your trainer about your and your horse's goals for the New Year.

I feel like my job is to inspire; a teacher has to know how to keep the group focused . . . I think that they have a very high expectation of me, and they know exactly what I expect of them. I think that that's what makes our relationship work.
—Andre Dignelli, top hunter/jumper/equitation trainer

With Your Horse

"Yes, you can walk down there . . . It looks like a big, green Astro-turf monster, but I promise it isn't. Wait, slowww dowwwn. You can walk. Yes, you can. You are fine. Easy. Walk. We are going straight. Go over into the corner, and forward. That's it. Good boy."

Is this a conversation that sounds even the slightest bit familiar? A new roll top is in the ring, you are sitting on your fresh horse, your lesson is about to start, and voilà—you find yourself giving an impromptu pep talk as you prance down the long side. Of course verbal communication is but one of the many ways you connect with those around you, including your horse. You are constantly communicating to your horse with your words (in your mind or audibly), your body language, your aids while riding, and your actions and behavior.

Communicating with your horse is one of the most enjoyable parts of riding.

The horse gets confidence from you when they're in a stressed situation. You have to use psychology when you're riding because horses are flight animals, so when they're afraid of something they want to run. You have to tell them and try to get them to understand: "You don't need to worry, I'm here." You've got to get [your horse's] confidence. You must speak their language. It's not up to them to speak your language.
—Debbie McDonald, Olympic dressage bronze medalist, first U.S. Dressage World Cup champion

Although this book focuses on the rider's psychology and preparation, the information you're giving and receiving in your relationship with your horse is ultimately your number one priority. Partnering with your horse has many intangible facets, but its overall quality is fundamental to your enjoyment, success, and motivation. It is your main objective to join with your horse to reach for certain goals, going forward into every ride united together in pursuit of excellence.

So how exactly do you get your horse to do the movements you dream up? Do you first explain a complicated exercise to your horse before going into the ring? Perhaps share an iced tea and kick some ideas around before your ride, drawing out your track on a whiteboard in the barn aisle? Not quite, but creating a relationship that includes a seamless and invisible line of communication between the two of you is something to enjoy and enhance with each ride.

- **Convey your plan, objectives, and focus to your horse in as clear a manner as possible.** You need to start with having a vision of what you want to create. Effective communication requires clarity and a lack of mixed messages. You can't canter your horse toward a big, wide oxer, take your leg off, start pulling on the reins, and expect him to understand what you want to do. Do you want to jump the jump, or not? You must instead maintain your clarity of purpose, be confident in your joint abilities, and have full access to all your physical and mental skills to achieve understanding with your horse.

A qualified trainer can help you develop the physical skills, aids, and techniques that allow you to guide and train your horse to understand how you want them respond. This assistance will be most effective when you are committed, know what you want, feel emotionally prepared to get what you ask for, and remain focused on the belief that good results will transpire.

- **Assume goodwill.** Horses are incredibly generous creatures; they allow their power, athleticism, and grace to be shaped into such a wide variety of activities and disciplines. Remembering your horse's ultimate willingness to partner with you is a terrific foundation to work from. That way you can always assume goodwill when you're communicating with your horse—either on the ground or on his back.

  When you work from a perspective that your horse is always trying to understand you and what you're asking, you take on more responsibility for the quality of the ride. Taking the initial perspective that any resistance from your horse (assuming his health and soundness, of course) is the result of a lack of understanding of your aids and ride plan will motivate you to be more clear and precise with your communication.

- **Acknowledge that your highlights came from teamwork with your horse.** As you recognize and enjoy the successes with your horse, no matter how small, think about how you both contributed to them. For example, when you have just done four-tempis across the diagonal for the first time, completed a smooth and balanced halt at the markers, or stayed calm and composed during a wild-and-woolly cross-country school, remember that it took teamwork with your horse to make it happen. This may seem obvious, but recognizing your horse's participation in a thorough way will solidify your trust in him, your ability to communicate, and your belief in your teamwork. In your Post-Ride Notes, you might write something like, "I said 'whoa' in every corner and he listened so well that I saw his ears cock back toward me a couple of times. It really helped him soften and stay more relaxed throughout the entire course."

By reflecting on the specific things you each did to contribute to the team effort, you create positive expectations that success can and will happen again (and again). These positive expectations will affect the quality of your future communication—when you expect success, you have better access to the skills (aids, techniques, methods) that help create it.

- **Use video and visualization to assess the messages you're sending.** Another valuable way to improve the lines of communication you have with your horse is to use video and visualization to check if the messages you believe you're sending to your horse are the ones you're actually sending. You may think you are sitting tall with your hands quiet as you ask for the counter-canter, when in reality your shoulders are rounded, your body is twisted, and your hands are almost in your lap.

As you watch the video, put yourself in the ideal position you would like to have in that same moment in the saddle. Imagine asking for the counter-canter again but maintain the balance and posture in your chair that you want to use in the saddle. This use of video and visualization will build and deepen your awareness, and therefore improve the quality of the way you communicate with your horse in the saddle.

I think the relationship is built by spending a lot of time with your horse. Riding that horse on a cold, windy day, riding that horse in a hundred-degree heat. Knowing their legs, knowing their feet, knowing their health habits. You can't teach that. You either want that to be a part of the process or you don't. You have to want that connection. If you want it, I believe that relationship is stronger and you can see it . . . and the rounds are better.

—Andre Dignelli, top hunter/jumper/equitation trainer

With Your Trainer

After completing an exercise where Scott made a sizable mistake, he looks down and then out of the ring, pursing his lips as Helen, his trainer, tries to debrief with him about what happened and why. Scott's nonverbal communication is powerful. It looks like he has shut down and doesn't care about what Helen is telling him; he appears stuck in his own negative cloud. To counter this, Helen talks louder in an attempt to get through to him, then sighs and puts her hands in the air. Suffice to say it is not going well, and like a snowball rolling downhill, the problem will keep getting bigger, and no one can predict where it will end up. Their communication stream is in desperate straights, and their rapport is obviously suffering as well.

Your trainer is a central member of your team. He or she communicates knowledge, guidance, and support on the little things (like a smile when you walk into the barn) all the way up to the major choices you make with respect to your riding career (like when it is time to get a new horse). Since it is such an important relationship, it is crucial to maintain healthy and open communication as much as possible. With so many people on your team and so much going into your riding, your relationship with your trainer is affected by many variables, circumstances, and events, and this is completely understandable. In addition, communication in the moment may not always be possible—for example, while you are in the middle of a ride—so it's wise to look for opportunities to be proactive and sincere when you can.

Working on trainer-relationship issues is rarely the main objective a new client brings to me, but keeping a strong and healthy relationship with one's instructor is so crucial that it is always assessed and often addressed at some point within the scope of my work with a rider. The following ideas about how to strengthen the lines of communication with your trainer were developed over my many years of consulting with riders; they're proven methods for enhancing and fine-tuning your ability to effectively communicate with such a key player on your team.

Andre Dignelli schools Maggie McAlary.

- **Use questions.** "Can you please explain that to me again?" (instead of "That doesn't make sense to me"). "Where do you see
  the most improvement?" (instead of "I feel like I never do anything right"). "What would you do about _____?" (instead of,
  for example, "I'm going to change my horse's feed program, find
  a new farrier, and bump up to Third Level next year"). Asking
  questions demonstrates your desire to learn and your respect
  for your trainer's expertise. It also starts a dialogue centered on
  gaining information and working together on a particular issue.

- **Express your commitment to improve.** Trainers always tell me
  that they love to teach riders who give it their all, work hard,
  and put forth 110 percent effort. They want to see that their

Stacia Madden gives last-minute pointers to Jessica Springsteen.

teachings are getting through to you and making a positive difference. They don't need you to be "perfect." They would, however, appreciate knowing that you are positive and invested. Show them your commitment—demonstrate it, talk about it, and display it nonverbally by paying attention and being attentive in your interactions.

- **Provide positive feedback for what works for you within their teaching methods.** When you let trainers know which of their methods help you learn, what makes sense to you, and how and why you understand them, it will boost the confidence they have in those teaching strategies. Your trainer might even do those particular things more! Do you learn best when you're given a moment to prepare before an exercise? Or when you're asked about what you feel? Let your trainer know.

Very often I also share my experiences. [Like] falling off at my first World Cup finals. I fell off in front of all these people on my birthday. My brain was like, "I am never going to ride again." Of course I went on to win a few weeks later . . . But sharing those experiences with my students [is valuable] when they feel like something is the end of the world.
　　　　—Anne Kursinski, five-time Olympic show jumper,
　　　　　　　　two-time Olympic silver medalist

- **Share your light-bulb moments.** Can you remember your last big "ah-ha" moment? You have just had a breakthrough in understanding the correct aids for a shoulder-in, you nailed a bending line the first time you rode it, or used a "greasy elbow" metaphor in order to allow your horse to go forward? Enjoy it! Share the enjoyment with your trainer and acknowledge the burst of positive energy you felt. Success is unifying, bonding, and motivating—all things any good working relationship needs a lot of.

- **Explain your process in "I" statements, not absolutes.** Saying "I am finding this difficult" is more effective than "This is impossible." When you're having a conversation or explaining your feelings, make sure you communicate that you know you can grow

Missy Clark walks the course with Hillary Dobbs.

and improve. I am told that there is nothing more discouraging than trying to teach someone who says, "I'll never _____." It negates the teacher's efforts because it assumes that no progress is possible, thus alienating the very person whose help you need the most.

I find ninety-nine of a hundred people respond better through positive reinforcement than negative. I know when I was a junior rider, one of my trainers was negative . . . I remember to this day how that felt, and how I really didn't feel like it was helpful for me. You definitely point out a mistake, you have to, but you also want to point out what they did well. It should be an unemotional thing.

—Missy Clark, top hunter/jumper/equitation trainer

With Your Non-Horsey Supporters

Spouses, parents, family, and non-riding friends who support your passion and encourage your dreams are also essential members of your team. These folks are not horse people, so they don't necessarily understand things like thrush and flying changes, but they care deeply about you and your happiness. They celebrate with you in your success and help pick you up when you feel down or discouraged. They're on your team because they support you in the multiple roles that you fulfill in your life, including your role as an athlete. How can you help them help you?

- **Define your supporters' roles and talk about expectations.** "I would love to have you come to the barn tomorrow and watch my lesson, _____ [husband/wife/best friend]. I'll be pretty busy, so why don't you bring _____. Would you have any interest in _____?"

You may appreciate the support you feel when close friends or loved ones come to the barn or horse show, but you also may experience it as pressure and a distraction if you feel responsible for keeping them entertained. They want to demonstrate that they care about you, learn about what you do, and might even appreciate an opportunity to help or feel useful. Talking ahead of time about what to expect and what they might like to do while they are at the barn is therefore a win-win.

To channel the desire you both have to make sure the barn or show visit will be a success, you can invite them to help with appropriate things to occupy them and let them contribute to the good of the team. For example, a role can be "Happy Self-Sufficient Husband Reading his Book/iPad While Occasionally Watching the Ring." If you say "I'm happy to stop before we get to the barn to get you a coffee, and please bring something to read. When we start jumping, I would be psyched if you watched, and I can explain what you saw on our drive home," you'll have defined his role ahead of time so you can both feel good about his attendance and independence, and promote the idea that his role fulfillment will help you stay focused and happy.

Solving Communication Breakdowns on Your Support Team

- **Reestablish a common understanding of the goals.** People in your personal life (family, spouses, friends) who are committed to supporting you as a rider are motivated to help you achieve your goals, but it's up to you to be sure they understand what those goals are and what steps are required.

It is also very powerful to reciprocate that support and give them encouragement on their aspirations. When you rally around important goals with people you care about in your life, you inspire all of them to bring their best forward and work together effectively.

- **Remind all your supporters of their contributions.** It's extremely unifying to tell folks often what you appreciate about their help, and how and why it is valuable to you.

- **Take some time apart to cool off if people are upset.** After a time-out, use a calmer approach so everyone can communicate more effectively. Knowing when to walk away and positively acknowledge a cooling-off period is a constructive way to regain your balance in the midst of a challenging situation.

- **Evaluate each person's role and brainstorm adjustments if necessary.** Communication problems may crop up not because people don't understand each other but because they don't like what they're hearing or the expectations placed on them. If a person on your team no longer feels good about his or her role, it may come out as interpersonal friction when it's really dissatisfaction and a need for a role adjustment.

- **Seek outside assistance when it's appropriate.** To gain an impartial perspective, you may find it helpful to include another person in a discussion. Also, a therapist or mental skills professional can help give you additional communication tools to create new strategies and solutions.

So whether your friend's role is "The Holder of Snacks, Carrots, and Water Bottle" and she is ready to dash over to you from her seat in the shade, or "Picture-Taker and Videographer Extraordinaire" sitting in the stands documenting the action, it is helpful to talk about what contributions you would appreciate. Have this conversation before getting to the barn or competition to facilitate a positive response, avoid miscommunication, and prepare accordingly.

- **Keep your supporters in the loop about your personal experience.** By communicating consistently and honestly about how your riding affects you as a person, you validate your supporters' care and empathy for you. They may not be able to understand all the technical, jargon-laden information you could talk about (for hours on end), but they still want to know how you feel and how your sport affects you.

  If a challenging day at the barn has made you feel emotionally exhausted, it can be valuable to tell a supporter the emotional content of your experience (without necessarily including all the specific details about fungus, broken martingales, and bit changes). This can help them better understand your perspective and prevent misunderstandings about your mood or energy level.

- **Share joyful highlights from your riding as well as challenges or stressors.** Explaining your joy at a goal you accomplished, along with the worry you have about bumping up to the next level, can help things feel balanced. If you only reach out to your non-horsey supporters when you're feeling down, they may get the impression that riding is mostly a drain on you and develop a negative attitude about your involvement.

- **Create opportunities to air feelings and keep the lines of communication open.** "How do you feel about me riding after work three nights this week?" "I'm thinking about going to the clinic next month. How can we make a family plan that works for everyone?"

Even the best relationships and communication skills can get stuck or go south from time to time. Fear about what you may hear can prevent you from asking loved ones how they feel about your riding and its impact on them and the rest of your life, but trying to remain in a "don't ask, don't tell" chrysalis state is not healthy for your close personal relationships. No plan, role, or boundary should have to remain static forever. Try to check in with each other periodically to make sure the supporters' role is working for everyone involved.

I think I had so much success because I had so many great people behind me—my sponsors, my husband, the grooms, everybody. It took everybody to make it happen. I think that was also very inspiring when you see the people that come behind you and really put you in front of them and say come on, you can do this. They have your back and no matter what happens, they're going to be there for you when you get done. Knowing that is a great feeling.

—Debbie McDonald, Olympic dressage bronze medalist, first U.S. Dressage World Cup champion

"As the Barn Turns"

Social dynamics at the barn can be fun, challenging, motivating, energizing, stressful, multilayered, confusing, entertaining—and everything in between. In fact, a barn's social dynamics can feel a lot like a soap opera. But unlike a daytime TV drama, you can't just turn it off when you're tired of it, because your horse lives on set!

Yes, the ups and downs that can occur when you get a bunch of horse people under one roof can be a bit mind-boggling, and over the course of your riding career, you'll be exposed to a wide variety of those situations. My best counsel on this subject can be summed up in two words: Pay attention! Without ongoing awareness and quality care, your interactions at the barn can affect your riding skills *and* your enjoyment of your horse. These seven ideas can help you navigate your barn relationships:

1. **Keep barn relationships in step with your motivation to ride.** Monitor the involvement, investment, and value you place on social interactions so you do not get pulled off course. For example, how much time to do you spend chatting in the barn aisle instead of caring for your horse? Are you happy with that balance?

2. **Protect your positive attitude by neutralizing negativity around you.** Hopefully your current barn has very little negativity, but truth be told, it can crop up in an instant when you least expect it. It is best to always stay conscious of outside influences on your thoughts and self-talk. You may not be able to change the people around you, but you can control how you let them affect you.

   Think about this example: Have you ever walked out of the grocery store singing a song you don't like? How the heck did that happen? Without realizing it, you absorbed the melody and synced up with it. This can happen when chatting with other riders too: Negative thoughts may unconsciously stick in your mind and become your own by accident. Be vigilant! Use positive self-talk, affirmations, and thought stopping if necessary.

3. **Model how you want to be treated and supported as a barn mate.** Ask for help, give thanks, offer your support, and explain ahead of time when and how the appearance of your support may change. If you are at a show and need some alone time as part of your pre-ride routine, you can explain that to barn mates in advance so they understand where you are and why you aren't clapping for them at the ring.

4. **Be careful about humor and sarcasm, in both what you say and what you hear.** "I had two pieces of cake last night—my mare is going to be hating me today!" Self-deprecating comments can have a very sharp edge to them. As well, being sarcastic and making people laugh is not a good enough reason to be engaged in a lot of negative thoughts and perceptions. Remember that your body is always listening, always trying to manifest what you say, believe, and intend. Stay committed to supporting yourself and being positive.

5. **There is an unlimited supply of riding talent.** No one else's skills take away from your mental or physical talents. Riding talent is not a rare gem, and there is no reason that everyone on the planet can't be brilliant on his or her horse—all at the same time! Therefore, examine what lies underneath your temptations to be critical of others and monitor how, where, and when you're tempted to say critical things.

Feeling critical and overly competitive can come from feeling insecure about your own capabilities. Be careful of this trap. You don't need to measure yourself against others to determine your own value, skill, or self-worth. Criticizing others to make yourself feel better or more competent will happen mostly when you don't give yourself enough credit for your own strengths, efforts, and progress.

6. **Use competitiveness wisely.** Pushing yourself to perform your best in a group-riding situation can be helpful, motivating, and energizing. Fantastic! Just be sure to balance your competitive drive to be the best by doing things like evaluating progress on your performance goals and keeping track of personal improvements.

7. **Get help when you need it.** Ask others for advice and perspective before handling chronically difficult relationships or volatile situations. Get other people's opinions on how to handle an interpersonal challenge, take time away from the barn to gain perspective, role-play difficult conversations ahead of time, and let compassion guide you when you are problem solving sticky barn-mate situations.

A TOP TIP

Riding is actually a team sport, and your ability
to communicate defines your level of success.

Chapter Highlights
Communication Skills to Build Teamwork

✔ Improve your interpersonal skills with tools such as active listening, lined-up verbal and nonverbal communication, and "I" statements.

✔ Enhance communication with your horse by being clear, assuming goodwill, and enjoying the teamwork you share.

✔ Keep interactions with your trainer positive and productive by using questions, sharing your light-bulb moments, giving positive feedback, and expressing your commitment to improve.

✔ For non-horsey family and friends, define roles and expectations, share challenges as well as highlights, and keep the lines of communication open.

9
Resilience

Use Mental Skills to Successfully
Adapt in Challenging Situations

Y OU JUST TURNED left when you were supposed to turn right.
Now you're getting an earful from your clinician. What happens next?

You found out you won't be able to buy the horse of your dreams
after all. How do you react?

A loose horse in the ring whipped everyone into a momentary
frenzy. It's over now, but you feel scared and your horse is still wild.
What will you do to regroup?

Do you remember the last time you faced a challenge? Was your
response, "Bring it on—I know I can get through this, and it'll make
me stronger and better!" Or perhaps (more realistically), "OK, I'm
going to figure this out and get through it." At least both of those
are certainly stronger than "Ugh! This is awful. I feel sick and I don't
know how I'm going to deal with it." Even though some challenges

are welcome (tackling an exciting, tough course) and some not as much (getting back into the saddle immediately after a bad fall), remember that all challenges promote growth, particularly when you frame the experience in the right light.

Amazing strength, creativity, tenacity, clarity, self-awareness, and confidence can be unlocked when you're facing a challenge. All these qualities contribute to your resilience: the ability you have to recover from or adjust easily in response to adversity or change. These positive qualities mobilize your very best and can bring out self-knowledge you may never have been able to access. By looking at your riding career with a long-range lens, you can see the difficulties you have faced, will face, or are facing with an objective point of view.

Think back: Did you sign up for every challenge you've experienced in your riding? Probably not. Did you control every what, when, where, and how of those challenges? Again, doubtful. However, do you always control your reaction and response to them? Yes. Are you also constantly looking to strengthen your abilities as a rider? Yes. When you take time to examine challenges carefully, you'll see that they can be positive change agents, even when they come disguised as fear, disappointments, and mistakes.

Like it or not, you need to accept that resilience is a riding skill. In fact, soon after you started riding, you learned the ultimate truth: to always expect the unexpected around horses. "Hoping" that those unwanted trials and tribulations won't come your way is simply a misguided use of your quality time and energy. Instead, you can be ready for them by taking inventory of your coping skills, polishing your regrouping strategies, and acknowledging and appreciating your growth as a rider.

All the mental skills in this book will help you face challenges and bring out your best. But the selection and use of those skills may change when you're up against potentially upsetting and unwelcome events. This chapter shines a spotlight on some common, difficult scenarios and provides strategies for getting through them with grace, resolve, and the ability to trust that they will make you stronger.

Adopting a "Jet Plane" Perspective

Before you develop new ideas to help you be even more resilient, it is advantageous to gain a positive, long-range perspective. Pretend you're in an airplane flying over your riding career. There are beautiful lakes, valleys, green plains, and lots of inviting, gorgeous landscape. Those represent the joys, successes, and love you feel for your horse and riding in general.

Now, notice and pay special attention to the large mountain ranges, which represent the big challenges you have faced. They're beautiful and dramatic from the air, and you can appreciate the obstacles they represent. Recall what it took for you to navigate them successfully. As you reflect, look for direct links to improvements in your strength that those journeys created.

- What were some of your biggest riding challenges?

- How did you navigate them?

- How are you stronger for having gone through them?

- How did each experience help you face the next difficulty?

Identifying the progress you made as a rider after getting through your toughest trials will help you in two ways: (1) You'll recognize that you get stronger after facing your challenges, and (2) you'll gain confidence that you can successfully handle whatever comes up. Examining your past with this perspective can reduce any stress about the unknown or the possibility of difficulties ahead because you accept that they're a part of your riding landscape.

Resilience in Action

Leslie Howard, Olympic show jumping gold and silver medalist, shares an example of her mental strength:

"At the Atlanta Olympics, my mare stopped in the first round of the Nations Cup. It was a very long five hours until I got to go back in the second round. She had stopped, and then a rail, and then time faults and blah, blah, blah. So I mentally had to dig in.

"I took her out for a little school after the first round to get her confidence back because she sort of lost it there. Then I walked in the gate in front of fifty million Americans watching, and I just had to make it happen.

"There weren't a lot of options. I just rode as hard as I could and hopefully the mare was going to respond to that, and that particular time she did. She could have thrown in the towel, no matter how hard I was trying. But unless I was there creating that sort of energy for her, it definitely wasn't going to happen.

"We jumped a clear in that second round [and the U.S. team finished with a silver medal]."

Moving Through Fear

Two riders were scared. One was terrified to do more than walk on her new horse, while the other was afraid to really go for it in a 1.20-meter jump-off. They were both being held back by fear, unable to ride to the full extent of their capabilities. Having occasional, brief moments of fear is understandable and natural in sport, but when it prevents you from doing something, like accomplishing your goals, it's important to carefully sort it all out.

*[Sometimes kids are] going Mach 11 in a jump-off or just
freaking out, and I feel that it's related to some version of fear.
Whether it's physical fear or a fear of losing, they want to win
so bad that they sabotage themselves in other ways. But fear,
followed very closely by an inability to focus or overexcitement,
is where I say it's time to talk to the sport psychologist trained in
this department. I'm not. I can try to help them with confidence
building . . . but that's when I especially say, "Call them up.
It's time right now."*

—Missy Clark, top hunter/jumper/equitation trainer

Step 1: Examine Your Fear

Fear is a little bit like the monster that lived under your bed when
you were a child. The more you pretend not to be afraid or try to
ignore it, the bigger and scarier it gets. When you look at your fear
clearly, you take away a great deal of its power because you realize
your imagination can make it much more frightening than it actually is. Turning the lights on and checking under the bed takes away
fear's strength, which is based on extreme worry about the unknown.
What will happen if _____?

"What if's" are the language of the fear monster:

- What if I forget my test?

- What if I disappoint my trainer?

- What if I fall off?

- What if I confuse my horse?

- What if my horse spooks?

What exactly are you afraid of if those things were to happen?
What is the worst-case scenario?

- Embarrassment?

- Injury?

- Mistakes?

Additionally, how does your fear manifest itself?

- Is it locking you up and making you tight?

- Is it a worried thought that comes and goes?

- Do you have both physical and mental symptoms of your fear?

- Does the fear help you in any way?

- Does the fear serve you?

- Does it help you achieve your riding goals?

- Is it making you a better rider?

These questions help you get to the heart of the matter when you're afraid. Your answers will better equip you to make a conscious choice to leave fear behind. Writing them down in black and white will remove the mystery and help you craft a thorough, effective response.

STEP 2: HARNESS YOUR MOTIVATION

Understand how to address your fear appropriately by asking yourself, Do I want to do what I'm afraid of? Things like jumping the tricky corner, schooling your horse when the ring is wildly busy, or getting back on after a fall? If the answer is no, then you need to talk to your support team to figure out if it makes sense to take a break for a while to gather your strength and desire.

If you say yes and you want to get through your fear, go a step deeper and ask yourself, What do I enjoy about _____? By shining a bright light on what you love and appreciate about _____ [the thing you're afraid of], you'll realize that what you want can be more important than what you fear. Make no mistake: This knowledge is power. At the end of the day, motivation can trump fear every time.

If something is causing you to feel afraid right now, ask yourself, Why is it so important to me to do _____? Think about your motivation: How does this particular activity fit into your overall riding plan and what do you like about it? If it's something you've done before, think back to a time when it was going well and brainstorm everything you enjoyed about it. If it's something new, use your imagination to paint a picture of the best it could make you feel. This motivation should be present in your day-to-day life—so write it down and post it in places you'll see on a regular basis, and make it real by talking about it with people who care about you.

I've been afraid twice while riding. Once when I was thirteen. A horse named Sox bucked me off, so I begged to not ride buckers every lesson after that. My instructor insisted I ride Sox for months after that. To ride, I had the choice to ride Sox or ride no one. This taught me that to overcome my fears, I must face them head-on. Then, maybe ten years ago, I had a young horse that reared. He was raring for a fight, so head-on didn't work; I learned that I had to be clever and teach him tricks to make him not want to rear. Thinking about what I had to do was a natural antidote for fear.

—Courtney King-Dye, Olympic dressage rider/trainer

STEP 3: SET GOALS AND TAKE ACTION
Fear can feel like someone has tied your hands behind your back with invisible rope, but that's an illusion. Remind yourself of what you control in your riding. Things like your focus, goals, self-talk,

energy, and communication. Then, take action! Shift your focus off your fear by integrating specific performance goals within your control into each ride. Empower yourself by crafting precise strategies that will support you in accomplishing what scares you. They can be very small steps, such as taking a Circle Breath before trotting around the ring without stirrups for one lap, but making some forward progress is essential.

By incorporating performance goals into each ride, you are saying, "I'm not going to sit around listening to the 'what if' monster. I am going to go accomplish x, y, and z." Fear thrives in an unfocused mind, so proactively focus on what you want to accomplish, not on the scary possibilities that fear has painted in the shadows.

STEP 4: ADJUST YOUR ENERGY AS NEEDED

When fear grabs on to you, it can trigger your fight-or-flight response, causing adrenalin to surge through your body. This can hamper your ability to communicate with your horse by contracting your muscles and affecting your breathing. It can also be a significant psychological distraction. If possible, brainstorm effective tools for adjusting your energy *before* you're in the midst of a fear-inducing situation. When your fear is triggered by something unexpected, it is also good to have a default response to handle your energy surge.

What have you used to normalize your energy level in the past? Chapter 5 discusses many tools for letting go of extra, unwanted energy. Try these: using breathing techniques, centering, doing a brief body scan, or channeling your energy into your performance goals. For example, a quick body scan can help you find and release tension before you begin something frightening with your horse. It can remind you that your mind and body have a positive connection, and that you do, in fact, have control over your coordination and energy.

Recovering from Mistakes

In riding, "perfection" can appear on the horizon as a tempting mirage, but using and believing in that term can distract you and damage your confidence. Indeed, the biggest obstacle to rallying from a mistake is the expectation that one day you won't make any. It's a fact: Mistakes happen. Medal-winning Olympic riders slip up occasionally—so do you and so does every rider you know. So what?

You're riding at an excellent level when you're effectively managing your errors in the moment. You may have caught the mistake early so it was imperceptible or it may have blown up into a doozy—in either case, you probably have something to fine-tune for next time. Once you have accepted that, you can embrace learning and recovering from your mistakes as a necessary and vital skill for bringing out your best.

> *If I publicly fall on my face, I go home and I work on it. I do*
> *the homework again. I come back out better. But you will not*
> *see me change my system in the heat of the moment. In the*
> *heat of the moment, I am the same. My demeanor is the same,*
> *whether I'm winning the class or losing the class. And I believe*
> *that has given the kids confidence and led to a lot of success.*
> —Andre Dignelli, top hunter/jumper/equitation trainer

My client Mark was forty-seven and had been riding for only one year. He had just bought a new horse and was heading to his first clinic. Let's just say that there was a lot of learning going on. As he put it, "I am certainly no stranger to mistakes. I just don't want them to kill my focus and get me so bummed out."

Mark was in no hurry to compete; he just wanted to be able to learn without throwing his confidence into the blender during each ride. I was impressed by his tenacity and enthusiasm for building both his mental and physical skills, and together we worked to improve his ability to get the most out of his mistakes.

HANDLING MISTAKES WHILE MOUNTED

When you make a mistake, like picking up the wrong lead, forgetting where you're going, or continually letting the reins slip through your fingers, it's essential to recover effectively and efficiently in the moment. With the proper strategies, you can not only get back on track, but also raise the quality of your entire ride. In fact, what you are (hopefully) doing right now—adopting a balanced, proactive attitude toward your mistakes—is the first vital step to coping with them while you're on your horse.

> *I tell them all the time to think forward. So the horse makes a mistake and now it's a rail down, or maybe you should have stayed out more in the bending line—just think forward and figure it out. If you build the skills of forward thinking into your practice sessions, it will come out in the [show] ring.*
> —Bernie Traurig, rider, clinician, and Founder/President, Equestriancoach.com

My client Mark was used to performing at a very high level in his other sports (running and golf). The learning curve in his new equestrian endeavor was especially difficult for him because of the volume of mistakes he made during each lesson, but fortunately, his motivation to improve kept him hungry for more.

We discussed how riding errors can be handled in a variety of ways. When you're schooling yourself or taking a lesson, you often have more leeway to stop and begin again. It is my contention, however, that this doesn't build the best mental strength or cross over well into a competition routine. Learning to regroup, refocus, and revise the ride in the moment post-mistake requires commitment and perseverance every time you ride, whether it is at home, in a lesson, or at a show. Here are the three steps in detail:

1. **Regroup.** The first thing you need to do in the wake of any mistake is to regain your composure and clear your mind. Use an exhale through your mouth to help this happen—release the tension created in the moment by relaxing your jaw and letting go of any anxiety in your body.

It's essential to recover from mistakes in the moment.

2. **Refocus.** Lift your eyes up and ahead of you to focus on the track you're on. Look with an active gaze, noticing details in what you see to help you connect to the present moment. It is easy to get stuck in an internal perspective after a mistake, becoming aware of your emotions, feeling frustrated, and replaying the error in your mind—all of which has a tendency to draw the eye down and make your gaze passive.

   This is also when integrating your performance goals into your ride will be an asset. Notice where you are and what is next and use a cue word like "Straight" or "Forward" to get you back on track and feeling proactive.

Let yourself recover from a huge mistake first, then investigate and learn from it to move forward.

3. **Revise.** Sometimes a mistake will require you to change your plan in the moment. When this happens, you must act decisively and confidently. Pick something—even something very small or basic—and go forward with trust that it will help you through a tough spot.

You can debrief your choice later, by yourself or with your trainer, but in the moment, it is more important to put your focus and your horse's on something positive you can concentrate on together. Particularly in a competition setting, a Plan B is an important thing to brainstorm before you begin an exercise, test, or course.

When Mark first started using this strategy sequence, the details of his mistake management looked like this:

1. **Regroup:** Exhale slowly through his mouth.

2. **Refocus:** Lift his eyes ahead and think "leg" to get anchored and maintain his new (lazy) horse's impulsion, as his mare often fell behind his leg.

3. **Revise:** Mark's default Plan B was "go forward," since he believed that most of his mistakes came from a lack of pace and positive momentum.

It doesn't do you any good to carry on and on about a mistake.
You need to analyze it, learn from it, and move on.
                    —Guenter Seidel, three-time Olympic
                              dressage bronze medalist

Processing Mistakes When Unmounted

Sometimes you're in the middle of a great ride, but then _____ [a big mistake that rocks your world]. You cope as well as you can in the moment, but emotions and adrenalin run hot. You are upset, shocked, and in denial, with your stomach in your left boot. To fully process this significant blunder, you'll have to wait until you get off your horse and let some time pass so you can review it more objectively.

Fortunately, your terrific habit of writing Post-Ride Notes (see chapter 2) will help you reflect back on a ride thoroughly and honestly. Let's be realistic: After a large mistake, you may examine it right away when you complete the course/test/exercise, look at how you coped, and figure out how to ride better next time. That's OK—you can review your progress and goals accomplished later. As you think back, recall both mental and physical factors that may

Another Mistake? Why?

Why do riding mistakes occur? Your and your horse's physical and mental skills, training, habits, as well as outside distractions and conditions all have the potential to be at the root of a mistake. The following are common mistakes that originate in your mind and then cause riding errors, or interfere with your communication with your horse. Be particularly attentive to these because awareness is a crucial step in correcting your mistakes—or preventing them from occurring in the first place.

- **Attentional mistakes.** These errors arise from not being present in the moment or being unfocused on the riding task at hand. A rider feels frustration at having a rail at the first jump in her stadium course and worries about the outcome of the competition. She is not prepared to ride the direct track in a bending line; her horse hesitates as a result, adds a stride, and has another rail down.

- **Faulty belief system.** Poor self-talk, lack of self-confidence, or a negative outlook undermine your abilities in the saddle. As you sit in the start box, your inner voice says things like, "Why did we come here? He'll never jump the corner. How many stops will it take to get him over it today?" These beliefs impact your behaviors, and limiting beliefs impede your skills.

- **Poor energy management.** At one end of the energy spectrum, we have "flat," and at the other, "extremely anxious"; both can take a toll on how well your mind and body respond to the demands of the task at hand.

- **Emotional turmoil.** Fear, embarrassment, doubt, frustration, anger, disappointment—as well as euphoria, joy, excitement, happiness. As we react to situations around us, these strong emotions can surface so quickly that we sometimes forget that we can control them *before* they cause any interference with our riding skills.

have contributed to your mistake, such as your use of aids, attitude, balance, and focus. Study it from every angle, as though you were solving a puzzle.

> [To recover from a difficult experience], it really helps me to get into what worked for me before, whether it's going to bed early, saying my mantra over and over again, visualizing, reliving the good things. Doing that instead of focusing on the bad [and saying to myself], "I did it before and I can do it again."
> —Anne Kursinski, five-time Olympic show jumper,
> two-time Olympic silver medalist

Understanding your mistakes gives you information to learn from and apply next time. For example, do you finally understand the link between looking down at the base of a jump and your horse stopping? Did you have a light-bulb moment about how letting your reins get too long encourages your horse to play in the corners? These are great breakthroughs to take to heart and focus on during your next ride.

With time, the new eventer Mark started believing that his mistakes might lead to fruitful discoveries, and he learned this system to help him process them: When a significant mistake occurs in a ride, do your best to solve it then and there, but also put it on your "solution to-do" list so you can go back afterward to craft the best possible answer.

Perhaps Mark could work through a mistake by repeating the exercise again and achieving success during the ride, or maybe it was just a tough day that didn't end with a tidy, excellent resolution. Either way, he took his ideas and his trainer's suggestions (if he had been in a lesson) and then added his own knowledge to his post-ride analysis. Mark examined everything he knew about why the mistake happened to craft a solution he would use the next time the same situation came up. If he had, for example, made the mistake of leaning forward and looking down to see if he had the correct lead every time he picked up the canter, he worked through it after his ride. The process of a "solution to-do" list looks like this:

1. **Ask why.** In Mark's case, he asked himself, "Why am I looking down?" He figured out that he looked down because he didn't trust that he'd be able to feel what lead he was on.

2. **Assess and acknowledge.** Mark needed to recognize that the mistake (looking down) wasn't helping him achieve his performance goal of learning to feel his leads, and it clearly was not helping him gain trust.

3. **Craft a solution.** Mark decided he would find a focal point at the end of the ring to hold his gaze on while he asked for the canter in order to practice feeling which lead his horse was on.

Mark also went one crucial step further: He visualized himself executing the solution. For example, he visualized five canter departures where he kept his eye up and felt the lead before he even tacked up his horse each day. *By visualizing the mistake's solution, you get practice riding it correctly and building positive habits—instead of getting stuck in error-laden memories.*

The next time you run across a tennis tournament on TV, watch what often happens immediately after a professional player misses a forehand shot down the line. When you see him step forward and mimic the exact swing and shot he just missed, he's imagining the shot going in. Mentally tough tennis players quickly and efficiently re-create a successful execution of the errant shot to leave themselves with a lasting memory of a success, instead of a mistake. Although riding does not necessarily afford you the same time to visualize in the moment, doing it after your ride is also very effective.

Picking out progress, highlights, and goals you accomplished will help you keep the good parts of a ride so you don't throw it all away when you also make some mistakes. OK, there was a beautiful round with one missed lead change instead of three? Progress! How did the clean changes happen? You chipped the first jump so hard it made the earth move, but got a forward, flowing pace for the rest of the round? Well done! Give yourself a pat on the back for getting mentally focused, picking it up, and flowing around the majority of the course.

In the beginning, Mark frequently let mistakes in an exercise destroy his opinion of the entire ride. Switching his focus to positive elements was a key breakthrough for him because it allowed his confidence to remain stable rather than being on a perpetual roller coaster.

It's over. It's done with. It's not your fault the horse ducked out at the in-and-out at a spooky ground line. There's nothing else you can do about it today. You've got to just focus on the next job to do. And you think about it at night: "OK, this horse stopped and threw me on the ground because of this, this, and this. So tomorrow, if I see that type of ground line again, or that type of situation again, I better handle it a little bit differently," and you figure it out.

—Susan Hutchison, U.S. show jumping team member

Handling Disappointment

It didn't go as you planned: Your horse was so lazy at the show; all your transitions felt like you were teaching an elephant to dance in toe shoes.

It didn't turn out as you had hoped: The barn you wanted to move into has a wait-list a mile long, and a landslide just ruined the arena at your second-choice barn.

It wasn't the outcome you wanted: You worked hard all year to qualify for _____ but it seemed that Murphy's Law was following you around like a shadow. A spook here, an abscess there, and your late focus on course led to some gaspingly long distances—it just wasn't your year.

How are you likely to feel about those situations? Survey says: disappointed. It's an understandable emotional response to not getting results you worked for, planned for, and did your best to create. So what is the good news? It is OK to be disappointed! Of course it is not a fun experience, but it is not all bad. Why? It shows you care. Disappointment is a result of your passion for riding, your horse, and the sport you love. This intensity is incredibly potent and can truly be a key ingredient for excellence. It is rare that you see brilliant performances executed by riders who don't have this level of enthusiasm for their sport. However, caring deeply about riding and bringing out the best in yourself and your horse is not without its risks, and one of them is feeling disappointed when things don't go as well as you had planned. What can you do?

Here are ideas for handling disappointment about a particular ride, test, course or show:

- **Remember you don't control the past.** You are a disciplined rider who focuses on things in your control; you spend your energy "controlling the controllables." Disappointment centers on regret you feel about a past event (such as a low score or jumping the wrong jump) that you cannot change no matter how bad you feel, or how much time you spend dwelling on it. It is therefore necessary to shift your gaze and concentrate on what is in front of you that you do control. And keep asking yourself, What's next?

- **Have the courage to put in quality preparation.** It is a protection mechanism to prepare haphazardly. You can safeguard against disappointment by being able to say, "Yeah, that wasn't so great, but I was sooo late today." Or "I didn't eat breakfast this morning and I just couldn't concentrate."

    By loading the front end of your ride with preparation you can stand behind, you'll be able to see your disappointments in a more simple light, allowing you to move through them more effectively. Do everything you can to create a good ride, and leave your best in the ring. Your disappointment won't be a long trail of missed opportunities and "coulda, woulda, shoulda's." Instead, it will be more straightforward performance issues you can sort through, set goals for, and work on the next day.

- **Set a time limit for focusing on your disappointment.** There may be sadness and frustration, or other difficult emotions that accompany your disappointment. They are understandable and the natural flip side of your investment in the process. (In fact, they are part of what allow you to feel elated and joyful when things go fantastically—again, they are the by-products of caring so much about what you are doing with your horse.) Having a boundary of time, like thirty minutes, or location, like when you leave the barn, can facilitate you switching gears to learn from the experience and move on.

Getting Over Disappointment
on the Biggest Stage

Debbie McDonald suffered a huge disappointment at the 2008 Olympics when her fantastic, beloved mare, Brentina, didn't perform up to her capabilities. Here, Debbie talks about recovering from that experience and the importance of maintaining trust in her priorities and process:

"[An example of getting over disappointment] was the last Olympics in Hong Kong. I still today think, my God, what in the heck went wrong there? That was never normal for her. I just had a whole different horse under me than I'd ever had in the show arena. Once I cantered in that ring, I thought, 'Oh, my God, this is the team medal.' There wasn't a whole lot I could do about it. I did the best job I could that night. Yeah, that's something I'll live with forever.

"When I got back to the barn, I was pretty down. I was pretty devastated there for an hour or two. I had great teammates, but I was still apologetic. I said, 'I don't know what to say other than I am so sorry.' What else are you going to say when you know you all didn't get the medal because of your ride?

"I had already come to the decision that after that competition, I was going to retire [Brentina]. A lot of people said, well, you really should come out one more time. I said why? That was her just being a horse. She has nothing to prove. No, that's it. I had made up my mind that was all she had to do and I wanted her to retire healthy and sound. I still have a horse that I'm riding every day and she loves what she does.

"I had to let that go and do what was best for her instead of trying to keep chasing that rainbow that was gone."

- **Be proud of your effort.** The outcome of a ride may not have been to your liking, but acknowledging and picking out specific examples of the quality effort you put forth can assist you in processing and letting go of disappointment. Own the effort you put into your sport, like your preparation, overall focus, energy level, and management of your ride plan—all the essential factors within your control that will play a role in your future success.

- **Use forgiveness, patience, and compassion with yourself.** Forgiveness can be extremely difficult after a particularly heartbreaking disappointment. Again, assume goodwill with not only your horse but also yourself. You both did your best. Being overly hard on the two of you, or your trainer and supporters won't help the situation. Showing yourself compassion and understanding is the best way to maintain your confidence and stabilize your attitude.

- **Maintain a balanced perspective of your long-term progress.** Amazing successes will happen in your riding, so will very frustrating letdowns. It's the nature of the sport. Watch your career as a rider; overall there is always forward progress, learning, and better awareness—even if there are momentary setbacks.

And ideas for handling disappointment about a horse-related circumstance:

- **Adjust your goals to help yourself adapt.** The saying "Change is all that's constant" holds very true in anything to do with horses. Your ability to modify and craft new goals to fit your circumstances is key in maintaining a healthy and balanced outlook with respect to your riding career and your recovery from disappointment.

Trainers, friends, and family can all help you be proud of your efforts in the ring.

- **Get support by talking with friends.** Remember that you're not alone. After a big disappointment, you may feel as though you're the only person in the world who has ever faced something like it. Airing your feelings can help you gain perspective and release the emotional response you have to the disappointment. And other people may suggest actions you can take to help the situation or get through it successfully.

- **Find something to look forward to.** Disappointment looks backward. When you can, it's valuable to start looking forward to something on the horizon that will be enjoyable and satisfying. True, there are no guarantees about the future, but allowing yourself to have hope and start putting positive energy into something new is a healing act.

I never get caught up in thinking what I SHOULD have done. I always just think of what's next. I have an innate ability to roll with the punches. People who've known me through the years

*remark on how unchanged my attitude was by the Olympics or
by this accident [a traumatic brain injury from a fall that left
her in a coma for four weeks]. I don't get too high with the highs
or too low with the lows. This goes with the big things and with
things as simple as mistakes in the test. I just think of what I
have to do next from where I am now.*

    —Courtney King-Dye, Olympic dressage rider/trainer

Coping with the Unexpected

They say that the best way to handle the unexpected is to expect
it. A nice theory perhaps, but who has the time to drum up all the
crazy things that might take place in a typical day at the barn or
horse show? Better to have a routine for recovering your focus by
directing it back to things within your control, creating and utilizing a Plan B, and adopting a strategy called "Notice versus Focus."

    Example 1: On a cold, wet morning, your horse has pulled a
shoe in the warm-up ring five minutes before you're supposed to go.

- Focus immediately on things you can control:

   1. Your communication. Ask for help for someone to call
      the farrier to their truck, and talk to the gate person to
      explain the situation.

   2. Your energy. Use tools like breathing and a brief body
      scan to prevent your adrenalin from spiking.

    Example 2: You have ten times more horse than you anticipated
today, and he's walking on eggshells.

- Go to Plan B:

   1. Adjust your goals accordingly and set new priorities, like
      smooth transitions instead of spot-on, accurate transi-
      tions, to redefine success and manage your expectations.

2. Quickly select one or two process goals, like exhaling in every corner, to help you both relax and cope with the circumstances.

Example 3: The eighteen-wheeler shavings truck that broke down outside the ring is waiting to get towed away by an even more mammoth-sized truck.

- Use "Notice versus Focus" to cope with the unexpected:

  1. Take one look to "Notice" and acknowledge the distraction (huge trucks, clanking, commotion) and assess what is going on.

  2. Control and narrow your peripheral vision to "Focus" ahead of you. Channel your energy into such things as listening to your trainer (if he or she is present) and managing your track, pace, and rhythm.

Remember, all riders need coping skills to flourish in the long term. Unexpected challenges aren't useless hardships; they are making you into the best rider you can be for a lifetime of enjoyment and success with your horse.

A TOP TIP

Just like pulling back the curtain to reveal the Wizard of Oz, demystifying your fears and challenges gives you greater understanding, insight, and strength.

Chapter Highlights
Use Mental Skills to Improve Resilience

✔ Develop the ability to use a "jet plane" (or long-range) perspective.

✔ Move through fear effectively by examining it, harnessing your motivation, setting goals, and adjusting your energy as needed.

✔ Regroup, refocus, and revise the ride to move through mistakes while mounted.

✔ To process mistakes after a ride, be sure you first understand what happened, then craft a "solution to-do" list, visualize the solution, and pick out some positive aspects of the ride.

✔ Work through disappointments about a particular ride by remembering you don't control the past, showing compassion for yourself, and putting a boundary on how long you'll let yourself feel frustrated.

✔ Value your efforts and stay aware of your overall progress to handle challenging outcomes.

10

Competing

Bring Your Best to the Show

WHEN IT COMES to competition, the goal of sport psychology is not to have you think more or follow a big to-do list. It's actually to get you to a point where you can think less. When you walk into the ring, your mental skills ideally help you trust yourself, your horse, and your plan, allowing you to ride with feel and stay in the moment. Your psychological tools may already be helping you do this at home, in your lessons, and schools—now it's time to make sure this happens at your shows!

In truth, here is one of the most fascinating questions that the field of sport psychology continues to tackle: What can create a difference in an athlete's abilities in practice versus competition? In fact, it was this very question that started me on the path of becoming a mental skills coach. Why can some athletes step it up and perform at an even higher level when they compete, while others perform far below what they are capable of in practice? Still others are very solid, but continuously deal with random, unexpected mistakes due to all sorts of factors ranging from distractions, nervousness, or self-imposed pressure. In equestrian sport you have the added issue of competing with an animal, your teammate, which of course adds some very unique factors into the mix of your competitive circumstances. The focus is on you, but how your horse responds to the show environment will greatly impact your performance.

What do you think makes the difference between a rider's capabilities at home and at a show, and where do you fit in? How do you handle competition challenges psychologically and how does that affect your physical capabilities?

Imagine this scenario and see how it feels: The alarm goes off and the sky is still pitch black. You jump out of bed, excited for the day ahead. You've been working hard at home, doing your mental homework, cross-training, and tracking your highlights in lessons and schools. Your preparation routine is dialed in for success. Your horse is strong, healthy, and happy, and has been consistently partnering with you on even the most challenging exercises. As you get dressed and gather your things to leave for the show, you are already directing the butterflies you feel to work for you, trusting that later they will help you achieve your performance goals.

Your attitude is powerfully positive; you are hungry to get in the ring to show what has been going so well at home. Confident and happy, you put the key in the ignition of your car and think to yourself, "I know today is going to be great. We're going to make it happen!"

Doesn't that sound fun? Can you feel the excitement to get to the horse show venue? In this scenario your partnership with your horse is on point and you know the momentum you're carrying as an athlete is due to both your mental and physical practice. Your training, ability, and mental skills will serve you at the show by helping you handle the ups and downs of competition as well as the intricacies of putting yourself on the line in an "individual" sport that we all know is really a team effort.

Have you ever been the rider in this kind of situation? If not, do you have hope that you could be in the future? Now that you're nearing the end of the book, you know a great deal more about how to bring out your best ride. I hope you recognize that the heart of what you have learned and polished is how to stay in the moment and trust your ability on your horse. These two factors are paramount to your success in competition. Being able to feel your horse, communicate effectively, and respond to the changing demands of the ride require mindfulness and faith in your reactions.

Although horse shows are a popular aspect of being an equestrian athlete, it is valuable to recognize that everyone's motivation and philosophy can be very different. In fact, this is an excellent place to start because your motivation and philosophy about competing can create greater achievements with your horse.

Your Competition Philosophy

What motivates you to compete? Things like having fun, winning, or being challenged in new ways? Ask a group of riders why they show and you are sure to get a wide variety of answers. Be that as it may, understanding your *own* horse show philosophy can help you make smart choices about your preparation, and help you excel.

To get the most from your philosophy, it is best to explore it in a proactive manner, rather than waiting for challenging, unexpected, or unpleasant situations at a show to trigger self-reflection on your reasons for competing. Three examples:

1. Your horse decides the monsoon-like downpour hitting the arena roof makes it impossible to concentrate on the jump in front of you, even though you are two strides away from it.

2. The bending line to the spooky skinny jump surprises both you and horse, even though you walked it four times and schooled it last month. This unexpectedly spirals into three stops and elimination.

3. You ride a beautiful beginning to your dressage test that unfortunately coincides with fighter jet pilot training above the horse show venue, causing your horse to come unglued.

These scenarios, somewhat predictably, can lead into the question, "Why am I even here?"

While it is often the challenges that can test you, and then crystallize and help you identify your reasons for doing what you do—I propose that you take a different track. I suggest being proactive and forward thinking with respect to your philosophy. Take this opportunity to remind yourself of why you compete, or get a fresh take on how you value showing.

Your personal philosophy for competing in your discipline will sum up the reasons you value it as part of your and your horse's program. For instance, if you hold the opinion that competing enhances your skills as a rider, then that is part of your philosophy. There can be many other facets as well:

- Seeing competition as part of your horse's growth and development as an athlete

- Using it as a method for charting progress

- Enjoying the people, social support, and validation you get at shows

- Traveling to new places, climates, and courses that keep you and your horse fresh and challenged

- Having fun

- Satisfying your competitive nature

As you read through these examples, you may find that some of them resonate with you. Create a list for yourself by including any of the above that apply and brainstorming others that may be completely unique to your perspective. Take note of your values and accept the way you regard your sport.

As you head to your next show, be aware of how your philosophy gets woven into your daily routine. For example, Sean, an adult amateur jumper rider, had been successful for a long time in his division. He was routinely champion or reserve and felt pressure to continue his success (which he admitted was a pressure he put on himself). Instead of feeling excited and challenged at shows, he had begun to feel a weight on his shoulders to "uphold his horse's reputation," and as we worked together, he became aware that horse shows just didn't feel fun anymore. This didn't line up with his horse show philosophy: to travel in order to take a break from work, enjoy his horse and his horse show friends, and continue to learn to be a better rider. Sean decided it was time to have a conversation with his trainer and support team to brainstorm ways to bring his enjoyment back to the forefront.

Horse Shows as Opportunities

If it is possible to recommend a philosophy, I suggest you add this idea to your thinking if it isn't already present: to see horse shows as *opportunities*—not exams to be passed or failed, but opportunities to create wonderful, connected rides that happen to occur in front of an audience. This gives you the ability to look into the pristinely groomed ring at zero-dark-hundred hours when you first get to the show and say to yourself, "Great, a beautiful, blank canvas on which to paint."

You have been practicing, just like making sketches in a sketchbook, and now you have the opportunity to create a fantastic ride in vivid color. With this as part of your philosophy, you relish each ride you have at the show, happy to present your and your horse's talents to whoever would like to watch.

HORSE SHOWS PROVIDE INFORMATION
Another philosophy to consider folding into your overall view of horse showing is that how you and your horse perform, what color ribbon you do or don't get, and what others think about your ride do nothing more than provide you with new information. There is no grand judgment being leveled upon you that speaks with absolute power and authority over you, your ability, and your future. No one experience in the show ring defines your potential or the value you get from the experience. You get to decide how to use this new information.

Hopefully you can sift through your experiences, gain perspective by taking mental notes or Post-Ride Notes to reflect on it, and then make wise and healthy choices about what to take to heart.

Every Olympics I have ridden, every horse I have ridden, every time I look back, I think, "If I had known then what I know now, I could have done better." Even though I was successful, there were so many things I could have improved. So I look forward to every show and every time to make things a little better, show it a little better.

—Guenter Seidel, three-time Olympic
dressage bronze medalist

Pack Your Best Mental Skills

So this weekend's show is right around the corner. What should you pack? Your mental skills, of course! Even though you're riding at home with terrific psychological habits (right?), it is always helpful to highlight, refresh, and integrate the specific skills you'll be taking to the show with you. In effect, you'll be "packing" them along with your show clothes, all your clean tack, and freshly washed saddle pads.

By now, you have experimented enough in your lessons, schools, and clinics to know what sport psychology skills work best for you, but you must remember to integrate them into your daily routine at the horse show. The categories below were presented in earlier chapters; take time now to review what works for you so you can pack them up and bring them along to your next competition. (For a sample mental skills packing list, see page 218.)

- **Confidence.** Set performance and outcome goals that are supported by clear, specific strategies for success; track your rides with Post-Ride Notes; utilize the "Two Positives" Rule when you finish a ride at the horse show to give yourself credit for your achievements (chapter 2).

- **Focus.** Know and concentrate on the things within your control; transform performance goals into cue words to utilize them in the saddle efficiently; use checkpoints within your ride and course plans to have a clear direction for your focus (chapter 3).

- **Vision.** Create vivid, controlled visualizations of your rides and courses; productively watch riders you admire; use the Outside-In Principle of adopting the posture and position qualities you want to possess (chapter 4).

What to Prepare, Organize, and Bring

A Sample Mental Skills Packing List for the Show

Everyone has a packing routine when leaving for a competition; there is so much to do and so many things to organize. Having a checklist for equipment, supplies, and feed can be a useful way to remember all the important details. You can also have a checklist of sorts to help you take your mental strengths on the road. Of course every rider is different, and through practice and experimentation, you'll fine-tune your own list. Here are some ideas to consider:

- Create or refresh two to three performance goals and strategies for the show. Break each one down into a cue word for easy access and integration into your ride plans.

- Pack a cooler with a variety of food and healthy snacks you know will work for you in a competition setting.

- Make a new music playlist with songs that will get you energized, relaxed, or into your "groove."

- Bring items to help you rest effectively, such as books, magazines, games, or small projects that will help take your mind off horses during your mini-breaks and rest periods throughout the long competition.

- A set of blank Post-Ride Notes to record your rides.

- A binder, fresh pad of paper, or index cards for recording the course(s) and your ride affirmations or reminders.

- Your favorite tools to adjust your energy, such as breathing techniques, brief body scanning, and centering.

- **Energy.** Use breathing techniques to adjust your energy level; perform a centering visualization to feel focused and balanced; turn to tools like music playlists, warm-up and stretching routines, and your nutrition plan to highlight the "fun" factor every day (chapter 5).

- **Attitude.** Assess and promote positive beliefs about your capabilities as a rider; maintain an upbeat attitude and set optimistic expectations for each day at the show; use your solution-oriented mind-set and focus on things in your control to best respond to challenges (chapter 6).

- **Preparation.** Utilize pre-ride routines that may include strategies for the night before you show all the way up to walking into the show ring (chapter 7).

Are you happy with your selections? Great! Now let's add some competition-specific strategies to use before you go and while you're there.

I think mental strength is the difference between who wins and who loses. I think that there are a lot of people with the same ability, but whoever is the strongest mentally ends up winning the classes.
    —Andre Dignelli, top hunter/jumper/equitation trainer

Positive Momentum on the Road

Betsy was leaving for championships in one week. Everything was going well at home, and she had been honing her mental and physical strength. To bundle up her positive momentum, she planned to accomplish a few things before leaving for the show:

1. **Ride with Positive Pressure by setting an expectation for do-ing something correctly the first time, to a high level of excel-lence.** To make this happen, she imagined and quickly visualized a snapshot of the show ground's arena while waiting to do an exercise in a lesson in order to get her "blood up" and dial in her level of focus. Betsy also schooled scenarios that mimicked situations she would face at the show. By using Positive Pres-sure in a couple of schools and lessons before the show, Betsy narrowed her focus and adjusted her energy to practice riding with a competition-level attention to detail.

2. **Set aside time to review past Post-Ride Notes to look for suc-cesses and highlights.** This helped her solidify her confidence and positive expectations by giving her concrete examples of her momentum. A great school yesterday, a fantastic lesson

McLain Ward on Sapphire at the 2008 Olympic Games.

two weeks ago—all her memories contributed to her positive outlook for the show.

3. **Watch videos of herself in recent rides and from her last couple of shows.** Betsy picked out moments where she was accomplishing her performance goals.

4. **Think through one or two of the riding challenges she had faced during her last show.** She then visualized how she was now riding through those solutions more smoothly.

Sport psychology increased my win percentage by 30 percent.
—McLain Ward, two-time Olympic
show jumping gold medalist

At the Show

You have flown, driven, or hitched a ride for a short hop or a great distance to get to the horse show—however it happened, you're there now and very excited! On any given day at the show, you have many things to attend to; at the top of the list is of course your horse. There are chores to take care of, and details for you and your horse's physical preparation, equipment, and logistics. Remembering to spend your attention and energy on those things within your control, you work through your day reacting and responding effectively to the many unexpected things that can also crop up.

When you turn your attention to preparing for the performance aspect of your days and getting ready for each of your rides, keep in mind that an organized, consistent preparation routine leads to consistency in the ring. These strategies are designed to take advantage of the horse show environment and the fact that you are often "on campus" for a long competition day.

RING RESEARCH

This strategy will help you acclimate to the arena, ring, or course before you ride or get to walk the course. Ring research involves walking around your ring or arena and watching from all sides to learn what it will feel like to ride there and how things are set. Because every venue is different, watching and studying from every angle prepares you mentally so you can minimize any distracting surprises during your ride.

Although you may learn horse-related training information from your ring research (for example, the ring may have a subtle slope and after discussion with your trainer, you plan to add leg going "up" the hill when you're on the course), my focus here is the psychological comfort and preparedness you'll feel from knowing what you're about to enter. Your horse goes into the ring with far less information than you do, and ring research helps you fulfill your responsibility to provide him with "rock steady" support and a clear, precise plan for navigating the new environment.

Preparing for your ride by watching from all sides of the ring can enhance your focus and confidence.

Doing ring research beforehand will also mentally streamline your course walk (if you are riding in a class that permits it), since you'll be able to concentrate fully on the technical aspects of your course instead of spending your time simply getting acclimated to the ring.

Walking an equitation, jumper, or show-jumping course at a hunter/jumper show or event is most often a finite process. You only have so much time to learn a great deal of information. When you give yourself time to do ring research and walk the perimeter of the ring beforehand, you will assimilate technical information more efficiently during the course walk.

[If time allows at medal finals], I usually ask [my riders] to watch from different angles in the ring. I always ask them to watch from behind the judges for a couple of rounds if they can.
—Stacia Madden, top hunter/jumper/equitation trainer

THE COURSE WALK AS REHEARSAL

The course walk gives you the opportunity to learn the technical details and physical realities of the course you're about to jump. It also gives you a golden opportunity to rehearse the physical reactions and muscle memory you want to have while on your horse.

For example, you may make checkpoints (see page 48) as you enter each corner on course to remember to sit up and lift your hand. Then you can mimic that reaction and teach your body how to respond at those places by lengthening your spine and bending your elbows as you enter each corner while walking your track.

You can also use time during your course walk to review such things as practicing looking ahead and through your turn while still staying out and walking your desired track. This will warm up your trust that you can look ahead while still feeling and managing what's going on underneath you.

BALANCING OUTCOME AND PERFORMANCE GOALS

To balance your goals, you first need to clearly identify them. On the Monday before a horse show, it is a good practice to write down your outcome and performance goals for the week. Let's say your outcome goal for a particular show is to finish qualifying for a certain medal. Your performance goals are using leg at the base of every jump (cue word "Support") and maintaining a smooth, fluid pace (cue word "Roll").

Both outcome and performance goals have their place, but be careful choosing *when* you think about each type. For example, people rarely ride well immediately after dwelling on an outcome goal or evaluating competitors' rides to try to predict the results of a class while they're competing. You will benefit from remembering that outcome is out of your control, and it can cause stress and worry when you remain focused on that type of goal.

Start your horse show day by mentally reviewing your performance goals and what you want to accomplish within your own rides. Allow yourself to trust that the outcome will take care of itself when you stay in the moment and meet all your performance goals. While it is understandable that your outcome goals will flash through your mind, it is very important to have a method for redirecting your attention to your performance goals—in effect "balancing" them in your mind.

Therefore, if an outcome thought like "I need to be in the work-off—I've got to make it happen" flashes into your mind, don't allow yourself to get anxious or be distracted; just switch gears and channel that energy into one of your performance goals or strategy thoughts. Replace the outcome thought "I need to be in the work-off . . ." by saying "Roll" to yourself and imagining you and your horse flowing through each corner. This will shift your awareness and concentration to a proactive, useful reminder of what you want to create in the ring.

I always did better not competing against anybody else . . . al-
ways doing my personal best. When I tried to beat somebody
else, nine times out of ten I'd screw up.
                    —Anne Kursinski, five-time Olympic show jumper,
                                    two-time Olympic silver medalist

VISUALIZATION

This strategy is worth repeating because its value cannot be un-
derestimated. When you're competing, visualizing before your ride
will lock in your ride or course plan by creating muscle memory and
training your focus. Visualizing with an internal, vivid perspective
will help you memorize the technical aspects of your ride.

Then once you're in the ring, you can ride in the moment with
instinct and feel. Not everything will unfold exactly as you imagined it, but your answers to the questions posed by the course, test,
or ride will be easier to access due to your excellent preparation.

The Warm-Up Ring

The warm-up ring may be large, inviting, and organized, or it may
be the size of a postage stamp, with footing that feels like a combination of packed dirt and beach sand carved into the side of a hill
(yikes!). Most likely, the warm-up ring you find yourself in on any
given weekend will be somewhere in between those two extremes.

No matter what the external circumstances, the next time
you're at a show, watch how riders handle the situation. Chances
are you'll be able to tell who is "owning" the experience and who is
simply "surviving." Your posture, facial expression, focus, and communication style will help you make that distinction. Do you think
those differences transfer to the show ring? If you said yes, you're on
the right track. Being comfortable and confident in the warm-up
ring will go a long way in creating those qualities in the show ring.

Focus on Performance, Not Outcome

Remembering her rides at the Pan American Games and Olympics, Gina Miles describes learning about maintaining a more personal, performance-oriented focus to achieve excellence.

"At the Pan American Games [in 2007], I was so focused on the goals of winning and getting a medal. I was so sure I could get a medal that I was really, even in the dressage warm-up, riding for tens and riding for the win. [I said to myself], 'I'm going to win, I'm going to win' and actually almost overtrained. Trained much too hard. Pushed for too much.

"[But at the 2008 Hong Kong] Olympics, my focus was 'I'm going to go and I'm going to give my personal best on all three days.' That really was the difference in my focus that time. And I did achieve a personal best in my dressage. I think I beat my prior score by six points or something like that. I really achieved a personal best there and had great cross-country, so that left me sitting in a really good position for show jumping.

"I didn't really look at the [show jumping individual] scores, but I did know that the top ten were all within a rail. I was lying fifth. Having the rail would drop me way down. And going clean would pull me way up.

"I obviously knew the information about the scores being so close . . . but every time my mind tried to drift there, I would bring it right back by changing my focus and going through the course in my mind again.

"I would replay it in my head, close my eyes, go through the course. [I would] feel myself riding the turn to jump one, then between jumps one and two—was I going to stay out a little here or how many strides is this?—I kept doing that all day long. Every single time I was tempted to think of the result, I would bring myself back to the process of how I was going to ride that course. And through that replay, I visualized riding the horse properly.

"A lot of times, especially for cross-country, if there is a jump people are scared of, they will visualize it going badly instead of visualizing themselves doing it well. They're scared of a fall or what could go wrong or the horse staring at the ditch, and they think about that instead of going, 'OK, I'm not going to let myself see in my mind it going badly. I'm going to make myself see in my mind how it's going to go well.' That was what I did with the show jumping [at the Olympics in Hong Kong]. I just kept visualizing over and over and over again.

"I could certainly not control whether the riders in front of me jumped clean, whether they pulled rails. That was totally out of my control. I could only control how I rode my horse, how I rode each jump and each turn."

If you're a rider who doesn't show a lot, then a simple lack of exposure to warm-up rings can make it a stressful experience. In fact, particularly tense and hectic situations can affect even seasoned competitors. If the mere thought of walking toward the warm-up ring makes your palms sweat and your heart flutter, then you will want to pay extra attention to mental skills that can help you start off on the right foot. Things like ring research, energy management skills, breathing techniques, adjusting your peripheral vision, and imagining show ring scenarios can be a big help.

There is nothing to be gained by staying in denial, dreading it, ignoring it, or trying to craft a meaningful warm-up that will take only forty-two seconds. Arming yourself with information about the flow of traffic in the warm-up ring, the subtleties of the footing, and layout will help you feel more in control and able to produce a positive experience for you and your horse. As you watch on foot, be aware that your stress response may be triggered. If so, take care to frame this as advantageous and do the following before actually getting ready to show:

1. Work through the adrenalin by talking to yourself: "I direct my focus and exhale my worry."

2. Use your breathing techniques: Take a few Circle Breaths as you stand close by watching to let go of the extra energy.

3. Imagine success on your horse: Do a short visualization ringside to imagine your horse softly between your leg and your hand for one lap of canter work.

The goal is for you to work through and minimize the anxiety you feel prior to riding your sensitive four-legged friend who will be relying on you to provide support, guidance, and purpose.

Everyone responds to the variable conditions in the warm-up ring slightly differently. You may be perfectly comfortable, or you may be fighting through anxiety that is cropping up due to the unpredictable factors in the environment. Either way, your ability to focus in the warm-up area is crucial.

When in the warm-up ring, you may respond to the busy atmosphere by narrowing your vision and looking down at your horse, or narrowing your awareness to an extreme. You may alternatively experience a hypersensitivity to what is going on near you such that you lose your awareness of your horse, your feel, and the refined communication skills necessary for creating a great ride. In this case, you're constantly scanning the ring, watching, and worrying about what might happen, and who might come close to you.

Both narrow and broad awareness are valuable and appropriate; it is key to have control over which you are using, and understand how to adjust them if necessary. Find the happy medium between a narrow focus and an overly broad one by consciously directing

Sportsmanship as a Mental Skill

I encourage you to remember one important fact about horse sport: There is enough talent to go around. There is also a lot of downtime at horse shows, during which participants watch "on the rail," a generally positive activity.

But it turns negative when you spend downtime criticizing and judging other riders' efforts. Why? Someone else's skills and superb riding do not diminish your own abilities. By being a good sport, and complimenting and admiring others, you can add to your own psychological well-being in these ways:

1. Giving credit where credit is due increases the likelihood that you'll also be able to praise yourself for you own strengths and accomplishments; this builds self-confidence.

2. Maintaining positive energy around you will certainly affect your relationships, including the one you have with your horse.

3. You will be using your energy wisely and staying focused on creating excellence. Never let your thoughts, conversations, or opinions about others distract you from your personal preparation and brilliant rides.

your eyes and peripheral vision, which are the best links to your focus, bar none.

To practice and develop control of your vision (and focus), use focal points as a marker for your gaze, then widen and narrow your peripheral vision when you first get into the warm-up ring. Choose a specific spot to look at, preferably at eye level and outside the ring if possible. A tree branch, the corner of a barn, or a particular place on the horizon works well. Next, widen your peripheral vision while looking at the focal point by noticing how much you can see to the left and right while keeping your eyes glued to your focal point. Then narrow your vision by deepening your awareness of just the focal point, noticing its color, shape, and location. This process will be a reminder and active process to help you control your vision and concentration.

Another way to fine-tune your vision and mental focus in the warm-up ring is to take a breath and expand your vision by actually turning your head, scanning everyone and everything in the warm-up while appreciating the environment. Next, shift your awareness back to you and your horse by exhaling slowly through your mouth, finding a visual target or focal point ahead of you, reminding yourself of a performance goal or cue word, and using a physical trigger such as rolling your shoulders back.

> In a warm up area, it can get really unpleasant because everyone is high strung at those moments. That's when you've got to take a deep breath and say, "The warm-up is 90 percent for the rider, 10 percent for the horse." If you can [say to yourself], "I didn't get as many jumps as I wanted or I didn't get exactly the warm up I wanted" but put it behind you, that's very important.
>
> I think a lot of riders really lose the class in the warm-up area when they don't feel like they've warmed up well enough. Really the warm- up is just to get the horse loose and the rider

Your Creativity

A Terrific Mental Skill for the Horse Show

Maybe you have always been keen to figure out special, personal preparation ideas that bring out your best riding at a show. Maybe your trainer or your friends at the barn inspire you. Maybe the mental skills in this book have sparked some great ideas you can't wait to try out at your next competition. However and whenever lightning strikes and you have an original idea about a way to get yourself ready, confident, and focused, be sure to grab on to it—you never know where you'll find a key to excellence.

Here are examples of creative ideas:

- Associating a particular scent or perfume with a cue word. For example, you can use the essential oil Mandarin (one of the top five aromatherapy scents associated with relaxation) along with the cue word "Relax."

- Choosing a song to sing in your head instead of counting "one, two, three, four" to maintain the rhythm of your horse's canter. "Row, Row, Row Your Boat" or any relatively simple song you enjoy can be a terrific choice.

- Writing down each course at a hunter/jumper show on one side of an index card, then writing affirmations and performance goals on the other.

- Wearing a leather-and-brass bracelet inscribed with the acronym that represents your motivation statement. "TAC" on a bracelet could stand for "Togetherness Activates Confidence."

a little bit loose and relaxed and then go. But I think people
. . . make it a huge deal [of it], and it's not.
—Laura Kraut, three-time Olympic show jumper,
Olympic show jumping gold medalist

The warm-up ring is really a fairly straightforward place: some room for flatwork, a couple of simple post-and-rail jumps, an area you can make into whatever you need it to be—at least in your mind. *Use your imagination to tune-up your mental sharpness in the warm-up ring by jumping jumps as if they were particular jumps on course, or doing a transition or movement as you would in the arena.* This could occur as a result of your trainer's instruction or be something you put in your mind while riding the exercises they have for you and your horse.

For example, you can rehearse your reaction and thought process in the air over the warm-up jump as though it were a jump on course happening before a tight turn, or as the first jump in a certain line containing a challenging question. As you approach the turn before the warm-up jump, set the stage for yourself by pretending that you're riding in the show ring, and as you ride through the corner toward the jump, ride it as you'd like to in the ring. Sometimes you can physically rehearse the turn or direction you'll take after the jump as well, although this depends on your horse's training needs, your trainer's plan, ring traffic, and other factors.

Maybe you jump a vertical in the warm-up ring and you sort
of ride that waiting distance because in the show ring, there's a
vertical-vertical in and out, and it's really tight. You practice the
feel you're going to want jumping into that in and out when you
go in the ring. Then you remember how that felt and go in and
do the same thing.
—John French, three-time World Champion Hunter Rider,
U.S. show jumping team member

"Notice versus Focus" in Action

A few years back, I had an eventing client, Drew, who was warming up her horse for her show jumping round (sitting in first place with no margin for error) when a flock of geese landed in a nearby field. Not a small, friendly number of geese, but an amazingly large, loud, and boisterous group of them. Apparently, they were so loud that it was even difficult to hear the announcer.

In our appointment following the event, Drew proudly reported to me that she told herself to use "Notice versus Focus" to stay focused on things within her control. She said she couldn't hear herself think with all the geese chatter. Her horse got wound up, and as Drew rode by her friend, she cheerfully called to her, "You're gonna win!"

Drew consciously "Noticed" these potentially distracting things by pretending they were just like cartoon thought bubbles floating by, and then actively directed her "Focus" to the productive things she could do in the moment. She paired the cue word "Forward" with a physical cue of opening her shoulders, shifted her awareness to feeling the quality of her horse's gaits, and got her eye up and ahead through each corner.

Drew went on to a clean round—and the win!

At the "Back Gate"

You and your horse completed a fantastic warm-up—you were both completely on it. Then you went into the show ring and rode conservatively and backward (and not in a cool, moon-walking kind of way, either). You came out of the arena baffled, a sentiment shared by your horse and your trainer. It's tough to know where things went awry. How did you lose your mojo? Something had to have happened between the warm-up and show ring, but what? The truth is that the moments you spend between your warm-up and actually walking into the show ring are delicate and require you to know yourself, your horse, and your ideal preparation process. It's necessary to tolerate some randomness with regard to what happens during those few minutes at the back gate, but you can take some steps to keep your positive momentum intact.

Let's investigate what often happens more fully: You find a great groove in the warm-up ring, you feel harmony with your horse (who is wonderfully on the aids), you are both focused in the moment, and then . . . you go into a holding pattern. There are actually two potential transitions that can be tricky to navigate between your warm-up and the show ring. The first is shifting from riding in the warm-up with great awareness of your horse and your body to the more intellectual or analytical job of talking to your ground help and thinking about your plan. The second transition is then getting right back into your groove by shifting your awareness to your body, your connection with your horse, and your feel as you walk into the ring or arena.

To keep the mind-body connection up and running during these transitions at the back gate, the following list of ideas can help. (This is just a start—please be as creative as you can and track what works so you can easily replicate what you find helpful.)

- **Include the "how."** As you do your final review of your ride or course plan at the back gate, keep your active performance goals in mind, including how you'll get them done. This will help your mind and body stay "on the job" during your course review. You could come up with the following two examples by integrating your goal strategies and instructions from your trainer:

1. *How will you flow out of every corner?* By maintaining a
    light seat and riding from your leg.

2. *How will you keep your horse in tune with you for the trot
    jump?* Imagine yourself using your voice to say "Easy" and
    keeping your body tall.

These types of links will keep your body on task and listening to the plan as an active agent in the process, rather than
getting lulled into a role as a passive observer listening to a
mental to-do list.

Use the time between the warm-up and the show ring to review specifically how you will ride your plan.

Sport Psychology Skills and the Wise Competitor

Less Is More

Early in my consulting career, I had a client who took it upon herself to drastically up the level and volume of sport psychology techniques she employed while at a show. We had not been working together very long when she went to an important horse show and figured that if some mental training was good, a whole lot more would be even better.

When we talked after the show, it turned out that she had visualized for almost an hour a day, taken copious notes about everything her trainer told her, performed ten minutes of breathing exercises before each ride—let's just say the mental to-do list she made for herself was very, very long. She came back from the show and told me she hadn't been all that sharp and in fact, she was exhausted. No wonder!

As with all the skills in the book, you need to know yourself and what works best for you. For some riders, having several sport psychology techniques is effective. For others, just having one or two "thoughts for the day" of the show will be enough to set their focus and energy level. It's your job to experiment and tailor a routine that feels comfortable to *you*.

Taper Off

If you are a rider who practices a lot of mental skills on a daily basis, competition can be an occasion to truly streamline all your mental skills and efforts to save time, energy, and mental strength for your actual rides.

Just like swimmers who taper their workouts before race

day, you need to take care you scale back your efforts so you don't overdo your mental training the day before the show, as well as each day while you're competing.

Choose Quality over Quantity

With any individual sport psychology skill (such as visualization or energy management), doing less that is high quality can be much more effective than doing a lot of repetitions that are muddled, interrupted, or weak.

If you practice well at home, your psychological toughness will be so powerful you can be efficient and effective when it counts at a show. For example, consider taking just one excellent Circle Breath at the back gate before you walk into the show ring to set your optimal energy level, instead of five that are shallow and fast.

- **Use a transition cue.** Transition from "planning" (talking, thinking, strategizing) to "performing" (riding the course, test, or run) by using a transition cue. This cue is designed to get you in the moment, almost like stepping on the clutch in a manual transmission car. Shift gears from analysis mode to performance by using a cue like a Circle Breath or a cue word like "Now" to transition between analysis and assessment to your riding performance. You move from thinking to doing. This transition cue helps ensure that you aren't stuck in your head as you walk into the ring where instinct and reflexes are paramount to a quality ride.

- **Repeat a mantra.** "Time to shine," "Flowing and smooth," and "One decision" are all examples of back-gate mantras whose job is to summarize a main goal you have and give you something simple to repeat to yourself as you get ready to walk into the show ring. A mantra would typically come into play after your course or ride review as you wait your turn at the back gate. It's a simple way to give directions to your mind and body while helping you create the feel and focus you want to have in the ring.

[My] mantra was "Stay loose." That was a big deal because I would get sort of stiff and add [strides] a lot . . . I remember telling reporters a long time ago [how much I used the mantra]. "Loose to [jump] one" was often part of my plan. Now people notice that I'm a very loose kind of rider, but really that was a big part of [building] it.
　　　　　　　　—Anne Kursinski, five-time Olympic show jumper,
　　　　　　　　　　　　　two-time Olympic silver medalist

During Your Ride

The show ring is a time for trusting, using your instincts, enacting good thought habits, and communicating with your horse. Your ride plans and mental skills provide a stable foundation to base your focus on, allowing you to then react and respond appropriately in the moment during your ride. Things may not work out just as you planned, so the need to be flexible and adaptable is paramount. This is where your preparation and mental skills will allow you to be confident and trust your decisions in the ring.

If you integrate particular mental skills into your ride, it will most likely be a patchwork-quilt including various techniques like performance goals, cues, checkpoints, energy management, and focus tools. *Once you know the best psychological tools for you to use in the show ring, know also that you can adjust their volume in your mind as needed while you ride the course or test.* For example, Jill was a rider who had a self-proclaimed "amazing habit" of running at and then (often) chipping the last jump in her hunter courses, especially when the first six or seven jumps had been fantastic. She learned to turn up the volume of her counting "one, two, three, four" in her mind through the corners, particularly on the way to the last jump or line, when she felt a tempted to evaluate the round ("This has been awesome—just one more!") or think about outcome ("We could win this!"). Counting "louder" to herself helped her stay anchored in the moment, focused on the process of her ride.

In addition to the tools and mental strength that can help you stay in the moment, you may also need to regroup if you get distracted by something unexpected or a mistake that takes you out of the moment. To get back on track efficiently, it is helpful to (1) value recovery as a task equally important to any movement you and your horse perform in the show ring; and (2) regroup, refocus, and revise the ride (see chapter 9).

Everything you do in the show ring teaches you and your horse something about performing and responding to challenges. Do you unravel and let everything slip away after a small, medium, or large bobble? Or do you exhale and refocus on the task at hand? During your ride, stay committed to regrouping and continuing to the best of your ability. By doing that, you're demonstrating a real skill—just like asking for a flying change or balancing your horse for a difficult movement.

Regrouping effectively in the show ring does require all your mental strength, but it is heartening to note that your ability will improve with each experience. The time required to get yourself back on track will shorten (from a whole course to a corner to a few strides to a millisecond), and it will pay off when all eyes are on you.

Occasionally it is the very young pony riders who can teach us the most about how sport psychology can come into play during competition. Walking or trotting into the ring or arena to truly show everyone what they can do can be such a simple process. Shelby was just that sort of competitor; her attitude was so bright she was hard to miss in any arena.

One day when I asked her how she prepared to go into the ring, she just smiled and said, "My pony is the best. I totally trust her. Even when we don't do well, I know we both try our hardest and that is all that matters." To Shelby, "showmanship" meant being excited to get in the ring and "show off" what they could do. After a mistake, she couldn't wait until the next class to try to improve. Ideally, all your mental and physical training should allow you to come to the show ring just like Shelby—with the confidence to stay in the moment and let it be simple and fun.

> *You just go in and you ride the best you can ride, and when you come out, I want you to say, "I rode the best I could ride to-day." I don't care how many faults you have. I don't care if you have a time fault—I don't care about anything else. I just want you to go in there and think about riding.*
> —Susan Hutchison, U.S. show jumping team member

A TOP TIP

Winning is fearlessly and consistently
pursuing excellence every day, every ride.

Chapter Highlights
Bringing Your Best to the Competition

✔ Adopt a constructive horse show philosophy that includes seeing the competition as an opportunity.

✔ Bring your positive momentum from home rides to the show by riding with Positive Pressure and reviewing your Post-Ride Notes.

✔ Prepare for your ride by researching the ring, using the course walk as rehearsal, and balancing outcome and performance goals.

✔ Acclimate to the warm-up ring with observation, adjusting your scope of awareness, and using "Notice versus Focus" to prevent distraction.

✔ At the back gate, include the "how" in your final course or ride review, switch from "planning" to "performing" with a transition cue, and use a mantra to quiet your mind.

✔ During the ride, "adjust the volume" of your mental tools as necessary and recover from mistakes or the unexpected by regrouping, recovering, and revising the ride.

11
Returning

Getting Back to Riding
After Time Away

"I'M ACTUALLY GOING to the barn tomorrow morning for a lesson. I sort of can't believe it," Shelley said to her friend Tara.

"Wow, I didn't realize tomorrow was the day. How are you feeling about it?" Tara was happy for her friend and eager for it go well; she knew how hard the past several months had been for Shelley when she couldn't ride.

"Really excited! But also nervous. I hope I don't make a complete mess of it. I hate feeling rusty and uncoordinated, and I just don't want anything bizarre to happen now that I can finally ride again." Shelley quickly tapped on her head as if knocking on wood.

"Wait, how long has it been exactly?"

"Almost seven months. It feels like an eternity. Part of me trusts that it will feel comfortable and easy, and another part of me knows it will be a little strange too. This is the longest I've gone without riding in I don't know how long."

"You'll do great!" Tara said. "Just enjoy yourself."

"Totally—my number one goal is to have fun no matter what. I'm always too hard on myself, so I'm just going to stay focused on little goals like jumping a few cross rails. I have also been watching some of my old videos and doing some visualization. Even if the process is slow, I know I'll get it back together."

Returning to riding after time away is something that a lot of riders experience, but the process is not exactly the same for any two people. Whether a physical injury to you or your horse takes you away from your equestrian pursuits, or it is the result of time off due to life circumstances like school, college, marriage, children, or relocation, when you return to the saddle, and even the show ring, you want to feel positive and prepared.

After a Fall

Maggie and I ran into each other at a horse show, where she sat me down and told me perhaps one of my favorite success stories about returning to riding after a serious fall. She and I had worked together on and off for years, and even though our work had tapered off as a result of her cutting back on her horse show schedule, she had truly absorbed so many mental skills that helping herself through challenges had become second nature.

When we saw each other, Maggie told me the story about how her older, "been-there-done-that" gelding had performed an impressive bronco impersonation while out on a hack one day. She stayed on for the majority of his antics but was ultimately left in the dirt (and rocks) with a badly broken tailbone, a deep bruise on her thigh, and a sprained wrist. It was the first time in her riding career that she had experienced such painful injuries in one fall.

After four very unpleasant weeks, Maggie had been declared "ready" to ride by her doctor and physical therapist but was aware that she felt a level of fear she'd never experienced in her long riding career. She was worried about getting hurt again, afraid of her fear because it was new to her, and keenly aware that she didn't want to turn into a "timid" rider.

Maggie described how she sat herself down, determined and confident she could figure out some solutions to her predicament because of the faith she had in herself and her mental strength. She was proud to tell me how she then put all her self-knowledge and mental skills to work in creating her own "mental rehab" protocol, and she was right—it was

Take care when getting back on after a fall.

impressive. It even highlighted many key steps for returning to the saddle successfully after a serious fall. Here are the strategies she used:

- **Strengthening her riding muscles.** Maggie took a proactive approach to her return to the saddle by performing strength-training exercises at home and in the gym. She knew she would have lost some of her riding fitness, and she wanted to prevent any mental stress that might result from feeling loose in the tack. Maggie used her physical therapist's exercises, as well as her own Pilates, yoga, and strength-training experience to make herself a program that focused on core and leg strength.

- **Spending extra time with her horse on the ground.** By not staying home and away from the barn while she recovered, Maggie maintained her relationship with her horse, even though riding wasn't in the mix. They had a long-standing bond, but she had never experienced such a bad fall, much less from a horse she trusted so much, and she understood that the experience had affected her in a deep way. She groomed him when she could, took him for walks, and generally spent time with him in the barn to rebuild her trust and preserve their rapport.

- **Listening to her instincts about the first few rides.** She chose her favorite time of day to ride (late morning) and took steps to manage her horse's energy. Even though her horse was a steady-Eddy type, she lunged him for five minutes each time she got on for the first week—not because he needed it necessarily, but because it added to her confidence. Even more important than his resulting energy level was the fact that she believed in her decision *to* lunge him and acted on that decision without negatively judging herself.

- **Setting very small, manageable goals each day.** Maggie made sure that she didn't go into her first few rides with high expectations. There was no master plan that needed to be adhered to. While tacking up or getting on each day, she asked herself how she felt, set a couple of small performance goals, and acted accordingly. This allowed her to simply do whatever she was comfortable with each day and finish each ride feeling successful. The first day her goal was to keep a connection from leg to hand and trot one lap in each direction of the ring. These simple goals were well within her reach and helped give her something to focus on each day (instead of simply wondering about her horse's mood and behavior, common distractions when returning to the riding after a fall).

- **Trusting that her skill level hadn't changed.** Maggie knew that she was an accomplished, talented rider and that her painful experience hadn't changed her physical talents or riding skills. She was able to look at her recovery as another challenge within her long and adventurous riding career, rather than an event that had to fundamentally change her attitude and abilities.

Maggie's plan to return to riding and work through her fear was something she built herself to get through a difficult time. What helped her most was the awareness and knowledge she had about her own process for facing challenges. Maggie's methods may not work for everyone, just as everyone may not choose to use the same trail to climb up a mountain, but the principles she employed are a valuable illustration of the some of the best strategies for getting back in the saddle after a serious fall.

Years ago I was in the Jimmy Williams Futures class in LA, and I had some four horses in the class. I made a turn back to something and the horse crashed through the jump and blah, blah, blah, blah. I came out of the ring and got on the next horse to start schooling. Somebody said to me, "Wow, I don't know how you do that. You're not worried about the fall you just had?" And I said, "Well, no, because I know what happened, why it happened, and I don't intend on making the same mistake twice."

If [you don't] know what happened—I think that is what creates fear. If you make a mistake, especially if you get hurt, and you don't know what that mistake was and how not to make it again, then you have something to be afraid of. If you know what happened and you know how to fix it, then it's not a problem.

—Susan Hutchison, U.S. show jumping team member

PHILOSOPHY AND MIND-SET

Regardless of your riding level, when you return after a serious fall, you can experience fear and psychological as well as physical discomfort. Although it doesn't always happen, if you find yourself in this situation, it's important not to judge your feelings. Allow yourself time to notice the apprehension and when you're ready, ask yourself this basic question: Am I going to let my fear stop me from riding? If the answer is no, then you are all set to fully realign yourself with the most powerful aspects of your motivation. You can do this by revisiting the many things you particularly like about riding, such as your relationship with your horse, the thrill of a well-ridden exercise, or the challenge of learning new skills. Remind yourself what you enjoy by revisiting your motivation statement, or better yet, brainstorm and write a new one! (See chapter 1.)

The other powerful method for aligning with your motivation is reminding yourself that you are *choosing* to put your foot in the stirrup each day you go ride. Anytime you remind yourself that you have a choice, it's empowering. You recognize that your free will is in play and you're making a decision to act. Your motivation to ride momentarily wins out over the fear once you put your foot in the stirrup. It is then your obligation to stay focused in the moment to help create a positive experience for both of you.

When you embrace the choice you make to ride, it is healthy to also accept the fact that in every discipline of riding, falling off is a part of life. Sometimes you land on your feet and hop back on (and smile at your good fortune), while other times you may sustain physical or mental injuries—or both. The mind-set you employ in your recovery and return to the saddle can have a big impact on how the process transpires. Some of the best and most fundamental ideas are also good common sense, but like your mom telling you to have chicken soup when you aren't feeling well, sometimes it's helpful to be reminded.

- **Be kind to yourself.** When returning to the saddle after a fall or injury, you must be gentle with yourself. As you do regular tasks around the barn, like grooming or tacking up your horse, be patient since they may all take more time to accomplish. Being kind to yourself is a part of accepting the reality that for the time being, you feel different than you did before the injury or fall. Regaining your confidence and strength is a process aided by patience and acceptance; all your skills are still within you, they may just need a little extra time to come back online.

[When returning from injury], always follow your instincts. Always, always, always. If something doesn't seem right, just stop right there. Don't push it.
—Melanie Smith Taylor, Olympic show jumping
gold medalist

- **Get support.** You are strong, determined, and capable of returning to riding successfully, but that doesn't mean you wouldn't benefit from a little encouragement from your friends. Having people to talk to, plan with, and discuss the ups and downs of getting comfortable on your horse again will all support your psychological health and well-being.

  For example, one day a stray garbage bag may spook your horse, causing you to revisit feelings of fear and uncertainty. Rather than carry this experience around with you, ruminating on your frustration and anxiety, it is much better to talk about it, name your feelings, and get some support (as well as kind reminders) that you'll be able to handle these types of challenges. Who in your life can you reach out to in this type of way? Perhaps it will be someone who has gone through a similar experience, or a close friend who doesn't ride but who can lend an empathetic ear.

- **Ask for help.** "I would like some extra time at the barn today—can you please get dinner together?" "Could you video a part of my lesson so I can see how I'm doing?" "Do you mind pulling these bell boots off? My back is feeling pretty sore." Finding your confidence and returning to your previous level of competence in your riding is important, but there's no rule that states you need to do it all on your own.

You may think that asking for help is a sign of weakness, but in fact the opposite is true. Being able to solicit help from people who care about you shows wisdom and self-knowledge that bespeaks a dedicated athlete. Asking for help from your family, trainer, or friends can be a real testament to your dedication to returning to excellence in the saddle.

I've never been afraid after my accident. I got on a horse well before I could walk [again]. I'm glad I started so soon. Luckily, the coma made me forget everything, so I only knew I wanted to ride. Just getting on the horse . . . made me not question that they'd take care of me.

—Courtney King-Dye, Olympic dressage rider/trainer

THE QUICK RETURN

You hit the ground and exhale. After a couple of moments, nothing prevents you from getting up, so you do. You horse is there wondering what happened and if his job is done for the day. "No, we aren't done," you think to yourself. You can chalk this one up as a "good fall" even though it does take mental strength to get you back in the tack, focused, and ready to go again.

(*Please note:* If your physical health is in doubt at all, be sure to rest and seek proper medical care. These tools are to be used with the truly beyond-a-doubt moments when you feel safe to continue your ride. If at any time in the return to the saddle you feel pain, dizziness, or a gut instinct to not continue, listen to your body and call it a day.)

It's one thing to return to riding after a fall or injury has kept you off your horse for a chunk of time, but what about returning to the saddle immediately after a fall? Most likely, you have experienced this because falls are as much a part of riding as occasionally needing new stirrup leathers. It may not happen often, but you can pretty much count on it at some point.

In the past, when you have gotten right back on, what helped you regroup? How did you put the incident behind you and then focus on the task at hand? You may have been very successful at doing this, or you may have felt vulnerable and distracted as if riding through the middle of a herd of wild horses. When you get right back on after falling off, the goal is to create success or find a solution to a challenge, but often the fall has seriously affected your frame of mind. Use these tools to be mentally tough and focused when you're on your horse again:

- **Adjust your energy and realign physically.** Hitting the ground is always a bit of a shock, even when you gracefully land on your feet (and wouldn't it be nice if all your falls were like that?). Your energy may spike for a moment, and it's quite likely your body may need to rebalance. To regroup and get centered, take a Circle Breath or two and consciously loosen your limbs by doing rolling your shoulders and gently shaking out your arms, hands, and legs.

- **Figure out what happened.** If other people are present, especially if you have ground help like your trainer, you'll have assistance with this process. Understanding the cause and effect can help you release fear because you'll know more about how to prevent it happening again. Rather than getting swept away in your emotional reaction, try to methodically think through what took place. If unexpected behavior on your horse's part caused the fall, sort out specifically how you could handle it in the future, as well as stay on.

- **Choose one or two priorities.** Let's say your horse was fresh and when you used your spur for a lead change, he bucked, scooted, and got you off. You and your trainer may decide, for example, to take off your spur or lunge him for a minute, and this will be a physical training decision. By also selecting a couple of specific things to do and focus on psychologically, you can not only help prevent this from happening again, but also create a better outcome if it does.

  For this example, let's say you select the priorities of keeping your leg long and quiet with a deep heel, and continuing to look up and ahead of you. Those two actions will return your focus to what is within your control and may prove useful in both preventing the situation (in this case the buck and spook) and helping you stay on if he gets excited for the lead change again. Remember, choosing the priorities will be up to you, your understanding of the situation, and your trainer, but *the act of narrowing your concentration to just a couple of simple things will help you regroup mentally.*

After a Long Absence

Once upon a time there was a young woman who stopped riding by necessity when she was nineteen. She was sad about having to step away from the relationships, animals, and sport she loved, so she promised herself that one day she would return to riding. At forty-one, she was thrilled to realize she had the time and resources to start again. She happily began taking lessons and, for the most part, coped well when she felt out of practice or insecure. Soon she was leasing a reliable, friendly horse who had a terrific sense of humor when she made the occasional mistake. Her return was not without its challenges, however, and sometimes, after a tough day, she wondered if she would ever feel like a confident, talented rider again.

Although many things can take you away from your equestrian pursuits, whenever the time is right, returning to riding can be a real joy. Other life priorities such as children, school, career, family, finances, or relocation may have caused you to take a break, but no matter what the cause, your return to riding is reason to celebrate! Your excitement will create a wave of positive momentum that will serve you well. You can also help yourself have a smooth, successful return to the saddle by engaging in some preparation and strategies that can help you "wake up" mental and physical skills that may have been resting for some time.

REVISIT PEAK PERFORMANCES

Walking yourself through memories that stand out in your mind as highlights and joyful experiences will begin the process of rejuvenating your muscle memory and mental strength. Let's say you're returning to riding after a fifteen-year break and you find yourself wondering if it will feel the same. Probably not, but rest assured that you have habits of thought and movement waiting to be accessed. Yes, you may have held on to the old "bad" habits, but the flip side of that coin is also true: The very best skills you ever possessed are still very much alive and well.

Follow the same brainstorming process you used when creating your Motivation Statement (chapter 1) and write down memories as you think about your peak performances (see instructions on page 256). You may recall feeling anchored with a strong lower leg as you jumped your first big triple combination, or talking under your breath to your horse when you had a fabulous cross-country run.

Any memory you can revisit that you feel contributed to your feeling strong and competent can provide you with a helpful idea, skill, or attitude to use in your current rides. Think through the memories and then choose several specific items (such as "Anchor in heels" or "Use voice") to incorporate into your thinking. Write them down and put them in places where you'll see them often, such as in your tack trunk, by your paddock boots, in your car, on a bracelet—to be reminded of the positive emotions and strength they can generate.

Visualize Your Best Memories

Take the previous idea to the next level. Let's say you are over-thinking the fact that you haven't jumped a three-foot course in eighteen years, or done a shoulder-in or galloped with your friends across a field for the past decade. Take heart in the fact that you can jump-start your muscle memory by visualizing past riding events and experiences.

Once you have recalled some of them in detail, you're poised to ride through them again in your mind. Remember to use all the most important visualization basics (see chapter 4). You will also be assisted by old photos, music from that period, keepsakes—anything that helps bring you back to that time and place.

Think Small for Now

Additional ideas about returning to riding after a long, long time away come from the amateur-event rider Kevin, who was continually frustrated because his body did not act, respond, or feel like it did when he was younger. With a great deal of mental discipline, and a dash of sport psychology tools, he trained himself to stay focused on very small performance goals and appreciate the little things. At first it was easy for him to get stuck in his frustration because it had not been his choice to give up riding so many years before.

In looking at the situation, Kevin realized he had a choice: to leave the barn every day frustrated at what was not happening or start embracing what was improving and the fun he was having with the horses he rode. Once he acknowledged that his measuring stick for competence and progress had changed and let go of his regrets about the time "wasted" not riding, he was able to set appropriate goals—such as working on his balance and strength on the lunge line.

To help him appreciate small joys every day, Kevin used the "Two Positives" Rule (see chapter 2) not only as he finished particular exercises within each ride, but also as he drove away from the barn each day. For example, talking about his ride with his friends as they bathed their horses was a true break from the stresses in the rest of his life. Kevin noticed that he valued the camaraderie and carried a lot more relaxation and balance into the rest of his day once he left the barn.

When I had my first child, I was pretty much back riding in three weeks, competing in six weeks—that wasn't too bad. But with the second [child], the last time I rode [before giving birth], I fell off at a competition and broke my leg. Coming back from that was a heck of a lot harder from a physical standpoint because I was super weak.

I couldn't even post the trot. [I thought], "Oh, my God, I can't even ride. I can't even post the trot one time around the arena." So then [I kept] my goals very small. It was literally "OK, today I'm going to post the trot around the arena. Tomorrow I'm going to post the trot two times around the arena." I didn't think too far ahead. I just focused on "What do I need to do tomorrow? I need to trot twice around the arena. I need to trot three times around the arena." That really helped me come back.

—Gina Miles, Olympic three-day eventing silver medalist

Brainstorming Past Peak Performance Factors

During a peak performance, everything goes beautifully. You and your horse work together seamlessly, and you feel extremely happy when it's over. The following brainstorming exercise will help you identify the qualities, skills, and attitudes that helped you achieve peak performances in the past—even if it was the distant past. The events and details surrounding your peak performances should include things that . . .

- Kept you focused

- Increased your belief in yourself

- Strengthened your confidence

These factors will help link you back to your best riding skills as you return to the saddle. Here are the instructions:

- Recall a ride from the past (before your time off) that stands out in your mind as a vibrant, exciting memory.

- Briefly describe the experience in the middle of a blank piece of paper and draw a circle around it. For example, "Second round of the classic at Menlo, flowing pace, great decisions, so fun!"

- Close your eyes and visualize being in that time and place. No matter how long ago it was, think carefully through all the details you can remember. Use these seven questions to help trigger your memory:

    1. What did you do to help create the good ride?

2. Where were you? A ride on your own, lesson, clinic or horse show?

3. How did it feel?

4. What words describe the connection you had with your horse?

5. How did you prepare for it?

6. What were your goals?

7. What did you tell yourself before and during the experience?

- As you remember the factors (for example, "Spent time at the ring watching from all angles before I rode," "Took lots of deep breaths," "Told myself, 'Keep it simple'") that contributed to your fantastic ride, jot them down around the circle, filling up the page as you do so.

- Connect each factor or detail that helped you achieve this performance with lines or arrows to the main experience in the middle of the circle.

- When you finish, select two or three factors you feel contributed the most to your peak performance. The ones that jump off the page at you are the best candidates to select, highlight, and utilize on a regular basis. Once you explore two or three of your past peak performances, you'll have a valuable list of action steps. Of course you will want to freshen it as you create new highlights and positive experiences, but it will serve as a wonderful springboard for your return to the ring.

Back to the Show Ring

So, the last time you showed, did you (a) live with your parents, (b) ride six days a week, (c) wear breeches that were two sizes smaller, or (d) compete a few levels above what you are doing now? All of the above, you say? No matter! There is no better time to reacquaint yourself with what it feels like to challenge you and your horse, demonstrate your skills, and compete with your peers. But as you contemplate your return to competition, do the "what if" questions occasionally start swirling in your mind?

- "What if I don't have the courage to send in the entry form?"

- "What if I get brain-freeze right before I walk into the arena at the show?"

- "What if I embarrass myself, my horse, and my trainer?"

- "What if I don't feel ready—ever?"

Extra nerves or not, returning to the show ring does represent a significant reentry point into your sport. It is therefore worth putting in some extra effort and taking steps to ensure your success. (Yes, this means doing more than "hoping for the best.") It is understandable to worry that being rusty will prevent you from performing your best or, most importantly, enjoying yourself during your return to the show ring. The following six ideas are designed to give you a psychological boost and a smooth transition back.

1. **Watch video of yourself.** Current video (from lessons or schools) allows you to clearly identify the strengths you are going to put into use at the show, and old video—ideally from past show experiences—can remind you what you're capable of in competition.

2. **Normalize the show environment.** Resist thinking that the

show is so different from your everyday rides at home, since that will make it larger than life and more intimidating than it needs to be. The movements and skills you and your horse are performing, for example, are the same. (You aren't about to go to a show to ride a Second Level test and suddenly have the judge ask you to do canter pirouettes, right?)

Defuse the horse show in your mind by going through and reminding yourself of everything that will be comfortably similar to your schooling and riding at home. These include your preparation, your equipment, your use of aids, and your ability to focus in the moment.

3. **Write affirmations for success.** Writing current and up-to-date affirmations (see chapter 6) in the week or two before your show can crystallize your confidence and create quick access to skills you can rely on to help you at the show. Brainstorm your affirmations based on your successes in training, as well as on performance goals you'd like to accomplish at the show:

Most importantly, enjoy your return to the show ring!

- "I use my leg to actively support every transition."

- "I look forward to challenges."

- "I trust that we are a team—forward and positive every step of the way."

- "I stay centered and balanced to maintain our rhythm."

4. **Relish the process of having something to work toward.** Gearing up for a horse show can be a time of growth and development. As you and your horse practice for the challenges you will face, you build teamwork, communication, and trust in each other—potentially bringing out the very best in both of you.

5. **Focus on things in your control.** Recall the list you made in chapter 3 of all the things in and out of your direct control

Guenter Seidel on Aragon.

when you ride. As you return to the show ring, you may face many distractions that center on things out of your control. For instance, memories from your previous show experiences can disrupt your focus. They may keep you constantly comparing and contrasting then and now: You may feel like a different rider; you may be unfamiliar with new systems, routines, and horse show management practices; you are also (most likely) showing a new horse; you may be competing in a new division, discipline, or level. Phew, it's no wonder you feel like a fish out of water! By keeping your focus squarely on the "controllables" like your preparation routine, attitude, and communication, you will increase your comfort level immensely.

6. **Adopt a perspective of learning.** Help yourself get acclimated to the horse show by staying flexible and adaptable to new programs and routines. OK, it's been ten years since your last event. Yes, things have probably changed, but you don't need to prove anything to anyone or know "everything" just to get started. You will most likely be learning things about the horse show itself, perhaps building a relationship with a horse you have never shown and working with a new trainer and a new program. In addition, you may also be using new ideas and mental skills to help you prepare and ride your best.

   Embracing the learning process will go a long way to diffusing any stress response that would result from trying to be an "expert." Small steps like talking to your trainer and friends ahead of time about what to expect and going to observe a show or two before you compete can help you gather information about what to expect as you return to competition.

The first time getting back on [after a bad fall in 2010 that broke his pelvis] was a little bit of a weird feeling. I wasn't afraid, but it was just strange getting back on, especially on the same horse I fell off. Then exactly a year later, I went back to Germany to compete again. It was exactly the same place, same time that it happened. I kind of had a little flashback, but I was not going to let myself hesitate about it. And that was the best treatment—it was done in a second. It was just the initial getting over it. It wasn't a question of whether I could do it or not . . . it was like, just go on and do what you know you can do.

—Guenter Seidel, three-time Olympic
dressage bronze medalist

Whether you are returning after time away or have been riding consistently for years, enjoy each day you spend with your horse and appreciate the journey you're on together. There is magic in your partnership—relish every thrilling moment.

A TOP TIP

Returning to riding after time away is like giving yourself a present. Be sure to wrap it in kindness and confidence.

Chapter Highlights

Strategies for Returning to Riding After Time Away

✔ Spend extra time with your horse, listen to your instincts, and set small goals to have a successful return to the saddle after a fall has grounded you for some time.

✔ Adopt a productive mind-set and philosophy about returning to riding after an injury by being kind to yourself, getting support, and asking for help.

✔ Get back to riding well after a long absence to attend to other life priorities by revisiting past peak performances, visualizing your best rides, and appreciating the little things.

✔ Return to the show ring with confidence by visiting current and past horse show videos and photos, normalizing the show environment, writing affirmations for success, relishing new goals, focusing on things within your control, and embracing a learning perspective.

Bibliography

Andersen, Mark, ed. *Doing Sport Psychology*. Champaign, IL: Human Kinetics, 2000.

Benardot, Dan. *Advanced Sports Nutrition*. 2nd ed. Champaign, IL: Human Kinetics, 2011.

Garfield, Charles. *Peak Performance: Mental Training Techniques of the World's Greatest Athletes*. Los Angeles: J. P. Tarcher, 1984.

Huang, Al Chungliang, and Jerry Lynch. *Thinking Body, Dancing Mind: Taosports for Extraordinary Performance in Athletics, Business, and Life*. New York: Bantam Books, 1994.

Jackson, Susan, and Mihaly Csikszentmihalyi. *Flow in Sports: The Keys to Optimal Experiences and Performances*. Champaign, IL: Human Kinetics, 1999.

Mack, Gary, and David Casstevens. *Mind Gym: An Athlete's Guide to Inner Excellence*. New York: McGraw Hill, 2002.

Nideffer, Robert. *Psyched to Win*. Champaign, IL: Human Kinetics, 1992.

Orlick, Terry. *In Pursuit of Excellence*. 4th ed. Champaign, IL: Human Kinetics, 2007.

Savoie, Jane. *That Winning Feeling!:A New Approach to Riding Using Psychocybernetics*. North Pomfret, VT: Trafalgar Square Publishing, 1992.

Weinberg, Robert, and Daniel Gould. *Foundations of Sport and Exercise Psychology*. 5th ed. Champaign, IL: Human Kinetics, 2010.

Williams, Jean, ed. *Applied Sport Psychology: Personal Growth to Peak Performance*. 6th ed. New York: McGraw Hill, 2009.

Photography Credits

Equine Network would like to thank the following people for providing photographs for this publication.

Tarni Bell: xviii
Hannah Biggs: 58
Robyn McAndrews Burton: 242
Kindra Ericksen, One of a Kind Studio: 65
Carol Farrow: 3, 89, 138, 166
Erin Gilmore: 18
Hope Glynn: 41
Nancy Jaffer: 13, 21, 28, 52, 128, 150, 171, 172, 174, 220, 260
Tonya Johnston (author): 63, 72, 80, 101, 136, 158, 222, 235
Gail Morey: 113, 206, 259
Kaitlin Perry: 184
Ryan Anne Polli, Applehead Design: 26, 33,108, 121, 132, 152, 195, 196, 210, 245
Richard Raine: 50
Madeleine Todd: 36
USET Foundation: 96, 124

About the Author

Tonya Johnston is a mental skills coach and lifelong hunter/jumper competitor who specializes in equestrian sports. Working with riders in virtually all disciplines for almost two decades, she has helped clients attain success at every level, from recreational riders overcoming fear and anxiety to international competitors.

Tonya consults with individual clients, conducts mental skills clinics, and works with high school and university equestrian teams throughout the United States. She has presented at the U.S. Dressage Federation and the U.S. Eventing Association national conventions, as well as the Association for Applied Sport Psychology National Conference.

Tonya is a regular contributor to websites such as Equestrianprofessional.com and Equestriancoach.com. For four years she wrote a column for *Eventing USA*, the official publication of the U.S. Eventing Association; her articles have also appeared in a wide variety of other equestrian print publications.

A graduate with honors from the University of California at Santa Cruz with a BA in psychology, Tonya received a master's degree in sport psychology from John F. Kennedy University.

Tonya competes in the equitation and medals at "A" shows. She lives with her daughter and yellow lab in the San Francisco Bay Area.

CPSIA information can be obtained at www.ICGtesting.com
Printed in the USA
BVOW05s1534180416

444389BV00025B/233/P